BLEND

BLEND

CREATING A LOVING FAMILY
AFTER DIVORCE

Mashonda Tifrere

A TarcherPerigee Book

tarcherperigee

An imprint of Penguin Random House LLC
375 Hudson Street
New York, New York 10014

Most TarcherPerigee books are available at special quantity discounts for bulk purchase for sales promotions, premiums, fund-raising, and educational needs. Special books or book excerpts also can be created to fit specific needs. For details, write: SpecialMarkets@penguinrandomhouse.com.

Library of Congress Cataloging-in-Publication Data
Names: Mashonda, author.
Title: Blend : the secret to co-parenting and creating a balanced family / Mashonda Tifrere ; foreword by Alicia Keys.
Description: New York : TarcherPerigee, 2018. | Includes bibliographical references and index. | Identifiers: LCCN 2018018497 (print) | LCCN 2018034553 (ebook) | ISBN 9780525504498 | ISBN 9780143132578 (hardback)
Subjects: LCSH: Divorce. | Joint custody of children. | BISAC: FAMILY & RELATIONSHIPS / Divorce & Separation. | FAMILY & RELATIONSHIPS / Parenting / Stepparenting. | FAMILY & RELATIONSHIPS / Parenting / Motherhood.
Classification: LCC HQ814 (ebook) | LCC HQ814 .M3257 2018 (print) | DDC 306.89—dc23
LC record available at https://lccn.loc.gov/2018018497
p.   cm.

Printed in the United States of America
1 3 5 7 9 10 8 6 4 2

Book design by Daniel Lagin

To the Woman who raised me:
you are my rock. In you, I see God.

To my son, Kasseem, and his UNordinary love:
thank you for helping me remember who I am.

For my godmother, Patricia Soliman, the wordsmith
who inspired me to write.

FOREWORD

Dear Mashonda,

I am so proud of us. Prouder than words on endless blank pages could express.

I'm proud because at one time we both felt misunderstood by each other, and now, here we are: celebrating each other in this beautiful book you have written called *Blend*, which so honestly describes how blended families *can* work! It shows us that life brings us the lessons we need to learn, so we can share them and find ways to become more evolved and more conscious of how we love one another and create our lives in the world.

Through our process of successfully blending, I've discovered that "understanding" is the most beautiful word I know of, and yet, as a concept, it challenges us as human beings to allow the freedom of true understanding to bloom within us.

Swizz, you, and I have found real compassion by taking the time to stand in one another's shoes and accept that we are all growing and learning. We all play a part in the life we create, not only with our one-on-one relationships but all of us in the world together, for the love of one another.

When we can see each other for who we really are, as the three of us are doing, we can be free to actually know each other. Not just what we *think* we know or what we've been *told* but what we actually know with our own eyes, our own spirit; the truth that rests in the air around us and that is within us.

When I observe our kids, I realize more than ever that the love they see between us is the love they are free to give as well. Because they are one another's greatest teachers. Kasseem Jr. is Egypt's greatest teacher, and Egypt is Genesis's greatest teacher, so whatever we have taught them and shown them is what they will have the capacity to give. And that capacity is deepening and deepening with every conscious step we take.

I'll never forget the actual change I saw in KJ when he watched the completed "Blended Family" video with all of us together, which included pieces of our family—our grandfathers, grandmothers, mothers, and fathers, who have, through their own journeys, found their way to "blending." He saw us all, and *then*, he saw A$AP Rocky, and a light went off in his head, and he said, "A$AP Rocky has a blended family too???!!!!" He was both in shock and in the middle of such joy, as he realized that he was not the only one; that there are so many others; that we are not alone in this experience.

That is the reason I wrote that song, and that is the reason you have written this book. It is our collective hope that some lightbulbs will come on and shine brightly with the clear understanding of how blended families absolutely can and do work by inspiring healthy relationships for the millions of us who have the same family dynamic.

I love being a bonus mom (better known as Umi) to KJ. I love that I get to take him to his games and be a part of homework and other special school projects. I love how I get to gently show him how to have more patience when his younger brothers are driving him crazy, as I teach them all the ethics of how to play well together. I love how we collectively encourage him to find the words to express himself. I love to read to him and pray with him at night before bed. I love singing to him and talking to him about his crushes and helping him create the vision for his Halloween costume or any creative endeavor he is imagining. I secretly (and strangely) love falling asleep with my phone in my hand late at night, trying to figure out how to juggle all the kids' schedules, getting each of them the time they need with the adults in their lives to feel loved and supported. I love how KJ gives me a glimpse into all that is coming in the short future with his younger brothers. I love him so deeply and I'm so moved by his beautiful love for me. There are tough parts to this: the days when KJ struggles with living in two places, and when Egypt is sad because the big brother he adores is shouldering a lot of emotion. Sometimes when I have to work late or travel without my family, I feel guilty. And when Swizz is working and I'm alone with all the kids, I can feel them vying for my attention. Like most mothers, I want to be and give everything to everybody, and sometimes that's overwhelming. I worry about them all getting enough of what they need. But even with these challenging moments, I won't trade our experience. When I sit quietly, I know for a fact that we have all been brought together for something bigger than anyone could've ever imagined; something that we could not have done without one another.

I believe that's what all blended families are here for! But there is no manual on how to do it, rarely any positive examples, and barely any explanations or guidance on how to navigate those tricky moments that naturally come up on the journey to becoming a successful blended family.

But now, I believe there is.

So this book is not only for our family. It is for *all of us*! All of us in the world trying to stumble through life and its challenges with as much love and understanding as possible. For those of us who are looking for the way forward. It's for those of us who are *not* ready and for those of us who *are* ready to realize that *we* get to write the story of our life.

And it gets to be a triumph.

I'm proud of us.

We have triumphed!

With only love and support,
Your sister, friend, proud co-parent, and future Golden Girl,

Alicia

Sent with light

CONTENTS

INTRODUCTION

I n January 2010, my divorce from Swizz Beatz was finalized in a
New York City courtroom. Our son, Kasseem, had just turned four
years old. When my ex-husband remarried, my son gained a stepmother, Alicia. Soon thereafter, he was gifted with a new sibling.

At the time, I was not immediately prepared to accept this new
family dynamic. There were a lot of emotions that I had to deal with
first: heartbreak, denial, anger, bitterness, and, ultimately, fear. I ro-
tated through all those feelings. Around and around. One big circle.
I was damaging my spirit and stunting my growth. I was exhausted
by my own unhappiness. I wanted to be better and do better, but I
was stuck.

It was my son who pushed me to begin the work of setting aside
my ego and committing to improving the relationship between his
father and me. I knew that in order to be fully present, healthy, and
emotionally stable for my son, I would first have to accept that I was
wounded and in need of some self-love and -care. My child needed

me. I wanted him to perceive me as his nurturer and healer, not as one who needed to be healed from her past. I began to compare my childhood to my son's. I forced myself to remember things that I'd experienced growing up, all the lessons my grandmother taught me about life. And with that, I was able to put everything in perspective. I knew I had the power deep within me to change, to fix myself, to become whole again.

Once I found peace and stability within, I was able to create a bridge between myself and my ex-husband, and later with his wife. The three of us set the stage for real communication. When we were able to respect and honor one another, we were able to blend as a family.

EVERYBODY WINS

Our family is unique, but we are not alone. There are millions of families just like ours in the world. Almost 75 percent of the 1.2 million Americans who divorce each year remarry and create new family designs for their children. These are people who have been brought together unwillingly but ultimately need one another in order for their children to thrive emotionally. This book is about blending these families.

Is blending easy? Absolutely not. For my family, the passage of several years, a lot of inner work, and many open and honest conversations with Alicia, Swizz, and our son, Kasseem, were required for us all to begin working cooperatively. And the process is continuous.

The truth is this: Swizz, Alicia, and I don't always fully agree with one another or understand one another's perspectives and opinions. No three adults ever do. But we now know that we can agree to disagree and simply rely on the balance of acceptance and a good middle-ground decision.

Ultimately, when everyone puts in the effort, when everyone does the self-work, everyone wins.

You win because releasing unhappiness and discontent is always better than holding on to those feelings. Once you've healed, the amount of love available to be given and received multiplies because of the newfound love you will have for yourself.

You win because parenting is easier when former partners are able to communicate with each other freely and without rancor. Face this reality: when you share a child with someone, the other parent is not going to simply disappear. You will regularly interact with them during drop-offs and pickups from visits. You will often need to discuss and agree on important parenting decisions. Isn't it better to have these interactions be pleasant, rather than feeling as though a Band-Aid is being ripped off an open wound each time? (And yes, someone with whom you have a child can simply disappear. That absence negatively impacts your child and is the least desirable outcome.)

Most important, your children win.

In a blended family, children are able to enjoy love from all the people intimately involved in their lives without feeling as though they are betraying anyone. Children from blended families have more peace, more confidence, and a deeper sense of security.

We've all heard about parents calling each other every nasty name in the dictionary in front of their children. Or the parent who continually hauls the other parent into court over money or visitation. I'm sure you know at least one adult who will lambast the other parent while the child is within earshot. No matter how much a person may think they are shielding their child from animosity, it's simply not possible. The child soaks up the negativity, and it will erupt in some way at one point or another. Perhaps they will be angry and self-destructive young adults. Perhaps they will become master manipulators, have a debilitating fear of commitment, and/or be unable to trust people in adulthood. Some reports say that 41 percent grow up worried, underachieving, deprecating, and often angry.

With so much at stake, why wouldn't a parent seek to take another path, pursue another way? I suspect it is because they don't think there is an alternative. When you're in the middle of a breakup, it can be extremely difficult to see cooperation and friendship with your former partner or his or her new significant other as a future possibility. But it is possible. And given how many stepfamilies exist, we need a new paradigm of behavior. We need to learn how to blend. This book was created to help you become a parent who can save your child's future just by being an example of love and wholeness.

SHARING THE TOOLBOX

When I first got divorced, I was a woman in need of love, information, and guidance. That's why I'm sharing my journey. I hope that this book will serve as a toolbox for anyone who has experienced a breakup or divorce and is co-parenting with an ex. It is also for those people either married to or living with a partner who has children from a previous relationship.

In the first couple of chapters, I share personal experiences that will resonate with many women who have gone through a breakup or divorce, and I hope my triumphs will inspire you. I'll give you an inside look at the solo journey I took through deep oceans of my lost self before I eventually drowned my ego in conscious healing. I'll lay out my healing step by step—the parts when I used a therapist and the parts when I did the work on my own. Regaining your sense of self and your power is essential if you are going to be a successful parent and effective co-parent.

For the rest of the book, I describe how my co-parents and I came together to blend, and I share how our family works to maintain peace and cooperation. Swizz has written a chapter called "A Letter from a Father," and Alicia has written the foreword. Their unique perspectives are key to understanding our family's true story.

I've also included the experiences of other parents (some names you might recognize) who are walking or have walked a similar path. I interviewed several therapists and child care experts. Over the years, I've been asked tons of questions on everything from dividing holiday time and vacations, to encouraging the bond between siblings, to enforcing discipline in two households, to dating. Throughout the book, I'll present some of my answers to these questions as sidebars in a straight and unfiltered way. There are Reflection pages at the end of each chapter giving you, the reader, an opportunity to journal your thoughts and ideas.

No two families are identical, but my hope is that you'll be inspired by our template to find the best path forward for your family.

AN AWKWARD ROMANCE

The first time Alicia and I ever met alone, just us two, was in 2012. I had invited her to my son's sixth birthday party. She attended, and right afterward, she invited me out to dinner. It was a cute little Italian restaurant in SoHo. We met downstairs in the cellar, our own private area.

This sit-down had been a long time coming. We couldn't rush this encounter. To get to the point where we could sit across a table from each other, we had to respect time and allow some of the wounds to heal. We didn't know it then, but time would become our best friend in the years that followed.

We ordered wine and toasted to just being there. And then it got quiet. Very quiet.

I broke the silence first.

I thanked her for meeting with me and said, "You know, Alicia, I don't want to talk about the past tonight. Let's just start to figure out a way to create a healthy future, because one day we are going to share grandchildren."

I look back now and realize that it was God speaking through me in that moment. That one statement transformed our entire relationship.

Today I refer to Swizz, his wife, and myself as the "awkward romance"—three people brought together for reasons that were not always clear but who ultimately became the best personal versions of ourselves as parenting partners.

That night in the restaurant with Alicia will always be considered our "first date." We gave each other permission to slowly peel back the top layers of the armor that guarded our feminine spirits. With each hour that passed, we became more familiar with each other. And in every minute of our shared conversation, there was enlightenment. We saw things in each other that we'd never seen before. In that room, with no one around to judge us, we were the same. Two women with the same desire to love and be loved. Our voices had been heard by our own ears for the first time, and it was refreshing. We deserved that freedom. Every woman does.

That night, we joined forces to build a fortress around our family. We would never be able to deny who we were to each other again. Who would be proud of us? Our children, their children, and all the generations to follow. This mission was bigger than us. As women and mothers, we knew that we needed each other to successfully blend our family.

BATTLING THE EGO

We live in a society that is guided by false imagery and high-tempered egos that require instant gratification for short-term pleasure. Our culture has pushed us to invest more in outside appearances than in our authentic, inner spirits. Social media is a blessing in many ways, but too often we use it to hide from our own issues. It's very easy to get caught up in the gossip and drama that fuels media; one person's unhappiness somehow holds the power to make another person feel better about their own life. There was a dark time in my past when my dysfunctions were played out for other people's entertainment, when all the commotion of the public gaze fueled my ego and distracted me from doing the self-work. But once I settled in, I found the inner strength and wisdom to rise above public scrutiny and personal ego. So did my co-parents. We did it for the well-being of all involved, but most especially we did it for our children.

CHANGE THE SCRIPT

For too many newly separated couples, there is limited (if any) communication between parents. An empty stare at drop-off and an emotionless hello at pickup. Or worse: the dad rings the doorbell impatiently, the mother answers the door with an attitude from hell, and the small child stands there, eyes wide open, absorbing all this energy. It's a business transaction—a sour one.

> Is this the script you are currently playing out as a parent?
> Why do we do this? Because we are overwhelmed by resentment, hurt, and distrust.
> Who's feeling the negative effects most? Our children.
> Can we change this? Of course we can.

How do we change? We begin the self-work. We heal ourselves, and then we heal the relationships around us.

You see, the truth of the matter is inescapable: you can schedule
a visitation, but you can't schedule love. You can't schedule comfort
or happiness. Love, comfort, and joy spring up from intention—
deciding to put in the self-work and seeking an improved relationship with your co-parents.

I hope this book will help you understand that it's okay not to
follow the crowd, not to stay stuck in the patterns of behavior that
have limited you. I hope you can use this book to walk alone until
you've found yourself. I want you to awaken to yourself, your true self,
become one with your higher purpose. Once you accomplish that,
you can be anything you want to be. Your child deserves a parent
who is whole. Your child deserves to be supported and surrounded
by love.

Blending is about healing, letting go, and evolving. It's about giving yourself a true opportunity to be the best version of yourself so
that you can prosperously raise your children and nurture the relationships that are formed around your parenting experience. It gets
to the core, the nucleus of the situation and the souls of the people
involved. This is a journey toward creating a bond between self and
truth, between women and mothers, men and fathers, fathers and
mothers, and, of course, with our children.

BLEND

CHAPTER 1

Look to the Light

O n December 22, 2006, I gave birth to a healthy five-pound, ten-ounce baby boy. Swizz and I decided to name our son Kasseem Daoud Dean, which is Swizz's given name. The path to the moment of his birth was an eight-year journey filled with moments of joy, pain, celebration, and challenge. An obstacle course that no young woman would ever envision for herself.

The question I was pressed to answer was this: how do I begin to become the person I need to be for this soul I brought into the world? I thought I knew the answer, but life showed me an entirely different way.

IN THE VERY BEGINNING

Every blended family begins with two people coming together and sharing the cosmic experience of becoming parents. The connection might stem from love, a single desire to have a child, or a casual intimate connection. Whatever it was at the beginning, for many people the connection eventually expires. But in that original experience lies the foundation of the feelings you will need to successfully blend your future family.

When Swizz and I met in early 1998, I was twenty years old and he was nineteen. Swizz was sleeping on his father's couch at the time, and I lived with my grandmother only ten New York City blocks away. A mutual friend of ours ran a recording studio in Harlem. There was a picture of me hanging on the wall that caught Swizz's eye. He asked the owner to call me and make an introduction. We spoke on the phone for two months before actually meeting, but when we finally did, we became inseparable. Within months, Swizz was bunking with me in my small bedroom.

Together, we laid out a plan for our lives. Music was going to be our way out of the hood. We worked hard, with many sleepless nights spent at the studio. By the time winter rolled in, Swizz and I had moved into a two-bedroom apartment in Palisades Park, New Jersey. We hadn't been together for a year and still really didn't know each other, but everything we did together felt right.

Soon our hard work started to pay off. Everything around us changed. Our money was different, the people around us were different, and we started to see the beginning of what would become a music empire.

By the time we were twenty-seven, we were making a great deal of money. The previous year, I had a successful Japanese tour after releasing an international solo album. I was signed to a major publishing deal with Warner/Chappell Music, singing and writing for various artists while Swizz was pulling top fees producing records for every major hip-hop performer you could name. A few years earlier, Swizz had closed a label deal with J Records and signed me on as his artist. We were at the point where money didn't feel like an issue to us. We naively believed that our financial stability was all that was needed to start a family.

We began planning meticulously for the baby. We followed an ovulation calendar, did our best to avoid stress, even detoxed our bodies through diet before we began the process of conceiving. Two months later, we were pregnant, and we were both so excited. This new life was our only focus, and Swizz was an amazing source of support during our pregnancy.

BE OF GOOD COURAGE

I had imagined a sweet baby bump, with loads of pregnancy photo shoots, lots of shopping for cute little outfits, and an over-the-top baby shower celebration. The universe had a different plan for me. I experienced early contractions numerous times during my second trimester, and by the twenty-week mark, my obstetrician ordered a cerclage to hold the fetus in place. My cervix would be stitched closed in hopes of preventing a premature delivery.

I was terrified. Six years earlier, Swizz and I had become pregnant and I'd undergone the same procedure. But I'd suffered the worst possible outcome. I pushed my stillborn, with the cord wrapped around his neck, into the world he would never have the opportunity to know. This was our firstborn son. We named him Angel, and holding his lifeless, fragile body in the hospital room shortly after he died made me feel as empty as a smile that never knew love.

Now I lay still a second time for the same procedure, with a new doctor in a different hospital, pregnant with another life I wanted so desperately to bring forth. I steadied my focus on the young nurse's face in the frigid operating room. Her eyes were full of empathy as she warned me not to move as the needle was placed. The thought of a needle so close to my spinal cord immediately brought me to tears. I cried even more after the memory of my first son set in, but a voice within me told me to be still. So I was. I lay there, numb from the waist down, and allowed the work to be done.

Nearly thirty minutes into surgery, the clanking of metal tools quieted, and the doctor made his announcement: "Mrs. Dean, we're all done, and it looks beautiful," he said. I finally felt safe. The most important step to keeping my pregnancy intact was a success.

The security, however, was fleeting. Two months later, I had a series of aggressive contractions. I was admitted to Lenox Hill Hospital and told I couldn't leave until I gave birth. I was only six months pregnant. For two months, I lay there, day after day, unable to walk, shower, or even sit upright to eat. All I could really do was pray for a healthy baby.

Like the pregnancy before him, Kasseem was breached with the umbilical cord around his neck. The doctor told me I would need a cesarean in order to safely deliver our baby. Immobile on the operating table, I heard a slight cry, and soon after the nurse handed Swizz the baby wrapped in a blue blanket. Swizz placed him in front of my face; our noses touched. Our baby was warm and gave new meaning to the word "soft." He had arrived, and it felt like a miracle.

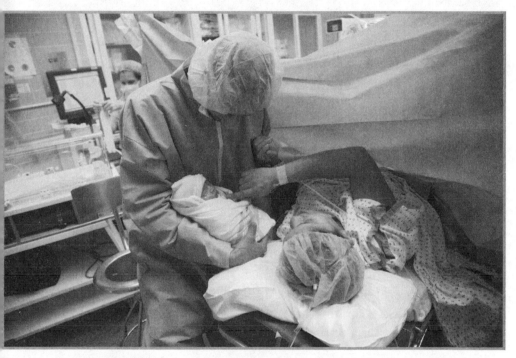

Every blended family begins with two people coming together and sharing the cosmic experience of becoming parents.

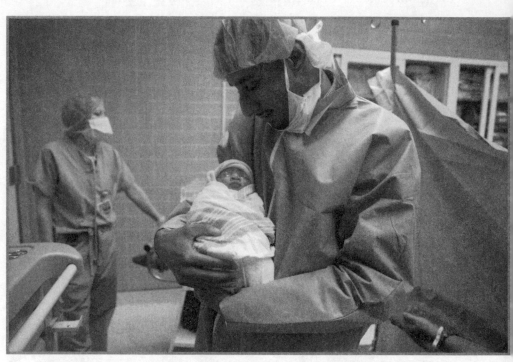

Because Kasseem was born three days before Christmas, I declared him to be my best-ever Christmas gift. Little did I know that he would unwrap parts of me that I never knew existed.

THE SHIFT

Because Kasseem was born three days before Christmas, I declared him to be my best-ever Christmas gift. Little did I know that he would unwrap parts of me that I never knew existed.

My son came to teach me a multitude of things about myself—things like patience and introspection. He would stare into my eyes, and it felt as though he knew his purpose in my life before I did. He knew I needed him in order to evolve as a human being. We hardly ever recognize our own character flaws by looking in the mirror, and often those closest to us have a hard time expressing what they see we need to work on. But something happens when you have a child. The physical changes are obvious to the eye, but what transpires spiritually is more difficult to define.

The moment I gave birth to Kasseem, I felt as though a new part of me had opened up to the world. The life I had been living for the previous twenty-eight years was now a memory. Before my son was born, I was a single entity. After that December day, another part of me, outside of myself, now existed. I would forever be connected to this new, tiny extension of myself, grown by my own cells, living and thriving outside my body.

My perception of life shifted. The only thing that mattered was protecting Kasseem. I spent that first year working toward being the best mother I knew how to be. I was completely focused on learning the nuances of this tiny human who depended on me for his life. I took being a mother very seriously. I felt a special obligation to honor him and his growth. I had made promises to God while lying in the hospital bed week after week, promises that I had to keep. So in the early months of his life, I started researching enrichment programs for Kasseem. By the sweet age of eight months old, he was already sitting in on music and baby yoga classes.

Once my miracle baby arrived, another part of me, outside of myself, now existed. My perception of life shifted. The only thing that mattered was protecting Kasseem.

Most new mothers worry about their child's diet and daily schedule. They wonder if the house will ever be clean again, if they will ever sleep through the night, or if they will lose the baby weight. There are also more intangible worries. Am I good mom? Am I doing everything I can do? We develop a picture-perfect vision for who our children will become and what our lives together will be. But that picture isn't real. It's sadly just the pressure society puts on mothers.

I had developed my own false image long before Kasseem was born. My parents had a messy separation and an even messier divorce, and though I was raised primarily by my grandmother, the time I spent with my parents was tumultuous, marred by instability and conflict. I never wanted Kasseem to experience the stress I felt. I was pretty clueless when it came to a traditional family upbringing with a mother and a father under the same roof, but still I wanted that picture for my son more than anything.

When I peeked out of the cocoon I'd built around Kasseem, I realized that things weren't the same in my marriage. It had fallen apart. First by small pebbles, then by larger rocks, and finally crashing down boulder by boulder.

Like a body in quicksand, my marriage and friendship with Swizz sank right beneath my feet. We had underlying issues of distrust and a lack of communication, and at that point, we were no longer moving as one. The heaviness pushing us under was stronger than our will to fight, and our ten-year foundation faltered. In only a couple of months we became enemies, unable to even look at each other. And just like that, one day we woke up and there was no relationship between us at all. We were only the parents of the same child.

WHEN HOLDING ON HURTS

I panicked. I wasn't ready to face this reality. I reached out to family and friends for help and advice. No one had the answer. No one really wanted to get involved. It got to the point where we were arguing constantly, and soon after, Swizz moved out. As I watched him load his belongings into a moving van, I could do nothing about him going. Now that we weren't together, there was a massive void. He had been the closest person in the world to me, and then he was gone.

Today I understand that we had to part. If we didn't, neither of us would have been able to evolve into fuller human beings. When God removes people and circumstances from your life, you may not be able to identify the reason for it in that moment, but the transition is always intertwined with a lesson, with growth. The more you resist the reality of this, the more you torture yourself.

Here is what I now know: no one ever belongs to anyone else no matter how connected people may seem. We all must live out our lives individually in order to fully experience our journey's purpose.

However, I didn't know this truth back then. I found the most comfort in being a wanderer, shelled up in my own skin of pain and confusion. I felt there was no one I could talk to; no one knew what to say to make me feel better. My grandmother lacked words for the first time in my life. She was deeply hurt for me, and I believe watching me go through this was a painful reminder of her own past disappointments with men. As a child I was her "baby girl," and as an adult woman I was her "dear daughter." She always wanted me to be happy, and for the first time in all the years she had spent raising me, I was completely lost in depression.

TOO MANY SEATS AT MY TABLE

Meanwhile, there was a relatively new phenomenon on the internet evolving months before the beginning of my separation—the gossip blog. This virtual reality of illusion mixed with human input happened to come along just when my marriage fell apart, and various celebrity-obsessed websites were working overtime at building their audiences based on new, hot topics. I clearly remember the first time I heard of social media. I was a bit in shock that people were actually communicating and sharing their lives with complete strangers through a computer screen that sent signals through the air. I resisted joining at first, but after Swizz created an account on MySpace, I felt I should do the same. We posted a few pictures of ourselves as a family with our new baby and shot an at-home piece with *Essence* magazine to celebrate our son's birth. At that time I never realized that the future demise of our marriage would also hit the covers on nearly every urban publication, blog, and website. There was even a mention on the *New York Post*'s infamous Page Six. Immediately I understood that society was more attracted to people's downfalls than their triumphs. Our separation became every trashy blog reader's daily cup of tea, and my life was sensationalized by the masses as juicy gossip to many.

I despised being called the estranged wife. Almost every single article I read about my life (and I read far too many) labeled me as the "bitter ex," the "baby momma," and, of course, the "estranged one." I've always wondered if all this would've been less painful if I wasn't divorcing a top producer. Would I have been able to move through the emotions of separation more easily if it had been done in private? Perhaps.

But I never had that privacy. It wasn't my reality. I had to deal with what I was served the only way I knew how at the time. Some women in the emotional state I was in bust in car windows or scrape their keys across car doors. I wanted to be heard. I wanted everyone to know that I felt awful, so I did interviews.

Lots of them.

I was a shameless sheep, exploiting my personal life, my family secrets, and my deepest soul experiences. I gave the public too much, and writers and producers sucked it up to get paid and to get clicks and views on their media platforms and networks. I gave too many people seats at my table. I didn't realize that this would one day be available for my son to see. I wasn't thinking at all.

Few women going through a separation will have the opportunity to spill their sad tale to an overeager reporter, but many women, when faced with the end of a relationship, will unload their miserable story to whomever is willing to listen. Their best friend, their family members, even a stranger in the supermarket. You want to be heard, to be validated. You want people on your side. And often, you're so wrapped up in the tell-all, so eager for support, you forget to choose your audience wisely. You pick people who will sympathize to your face and are then quick to spread the story as soon as you turn the corner.

Please don't misunderstand me. I'm not advising a woman going through a breakup to isolate herself and not confide in anybody. There are people you can trust, and sharing your thoughts and feelings can ease the pain. People like Sandra Dean, who is Swizz's grandmother and the matriarch of the Dean family. Granny, as she is affectionately called by all her family, has herself gone through a divorce after nineteen years of marriage. She was a thirty-year-old woman with six children ranging from age seventeen down to age six when she and her husband divorced. I spoke to her about her experience. "I had a great support system," she told me. "That's the most important thing. My mother, my father, my sisters, all my friends were very supportive. But they were supportive in a positive way. They never said anything negative about my ex-husband or our breakup. They only supported what I felt, what I needed, and how they felt they could help me move on."

However, even the people who want the best for you cannot give you the answers or solutions you seek. True healing is something you have to do on your own, a process I would soon think of as my lifesaver.

When you spread too much information, at a certain point you'll find yourself walking into the neighborhood coffee shop and feel as though everybody stops talking the minute they see you. My neighborhood coffee shop was the worldwide web. But I didn't stop giving interviews because my ego was running a marathon.

DEFINING EGO

What do I mean by ego? Ego is simply the opposite of love. It is the false self, the part of you that reacts to pain, that is driven by the external—things like social standing, money, and image. It masks the true self, that highest version of yourself, your spirit. When my marriage ended, something happened inside of me: fear entered, tucking my true self into a corner.

Ego is fueled by fear, and the result was an ego turned all the way up into full defense mode. A loud and obnoxious setting that no one but me had the power to turn down. Self-pity had morphed me into my own worst nightmare. A wake-up call was the only solution to regaining my peace. But at that time I had to get the need for validation out of my head.

I needed to be heard.

I had to voice my opinion.

I, I, I. That's what makes up the false self: the "I"s and the "me"s. I had to stop making everything about me and my expectations. This is the struggle that catches most newly single parents. The expectation that the relationship will last forever starts rubbing against the reality of the breakup. Clinging to what you pictured your future would look like pushes you toward a dark place. That certainly was the case with me.

THE LIGHT IN FRONT OF ME

There was a light in this scenario that I simply would not allow myself to see at first. The greatest light stood right before me: my son. And an even greater light was within me. I just had to do the appropriate work of mastering the ego in order to find it. It seems so simple in retrospect. All I needed to do was quit the self-pitying and let go of what was hurting me; then I could begin to look for the lessons in the sadness.

Ultimately, my separation and divorce taught me not to put the pressure of expectations on myself or others. Expectations are illusions. I'm not saying that we shouldn't want or hope for our partners to give us their best. However, the purest form of love is to allow life to develop organically, authentically, without the weight of expectations.

Expectations open up the doors to the "I"s and "me"s because it makes a situation about you and your ego. Empathy is the solution for an overgrown ego and eliminates expectations. It is also a key component of blending. We'll discuss how to rest your ego and embrace empathy in later chapters.

Sheree Zampino, who co-parented her son, Trey, with her ex-husband the actor Will Smith, offered a hopeful perspective: "Divorce is a death. The death of a relationship. The death of a family unit. However, you must let some things die in order to let other things live." Sheree is a Christian, and she told me that God's mercies are new every day. "That means there is something new for you. But not just for you: new for both you and your child." But no matter what your faith, what she said is something we can all believe. The end of a relationship must be processed for the death it is—mourned as a permanent loss. We also must allow ourselves to embrace a new path, to walk toward something that will bring beauty and purpose into our lives.

When I climbed up those seemingly never-ending steps to the New York State Supreme Court on Centre Street to begin our divorce proceedings, I was wearing head-to-toe black. I felt as though I were going to a funeral. And indeed a part of me had died. I felt like a failure of a wife and less of a woman. Insecurities ran amok. It was the end of the life that I had become accustomed to. It was the end of the life that I'd claimed as mine. I wish someone had told me what I now know: "Fear not. This is the first step to your new beginning."

CHAPTER 2

Rebuild Your Spirit

Blending is a brave yet humbling form of living outside your own comfort zone for a bigger cause: your child. In order to optimally blend, you must get out of your own way. On the road toward healing, I made some bad choices. You might find yourself in the same situation immediately after a breakup. Don't be afraid of this. Separations are never easy if the heart is involved.

FOR MY SON'S SAKE

During the separation and for months after the divorce was final, I was living life backward. It was like I was an adolescent all over again: going out every night, hanging out with women who dwelled in gossip and drama, and dating men who were completely wrong for me. I was trying to fill a void that could never be filled outwardly.

Kasseem was five years old at the time, too young to fully

understand what divorce meant. But he sensed that his life had irre-coverably changed. There was a large pool table in our living room. He used to ride his little tricycle around it over and over again. When Swizz moved out, so did the pool table. And it left a large vacant space in our home. One day Kasseem asked me, "Mommy, what hap-pened to the pool table?" Young children have very simple ways of connecting their emotions to their reality. And even though we may not see immediate, physical responses, they absolutely feel a loss.

I remember that Kasseem's eyes were filled with wonder and in-quiry, and I'm thankful that I found the strength and grace to give him a careful answer with a gentle voice. I told him, "Daddy has a new home. That's where the pool table is, and you will visit with him there soon."

During a separation, the adult must quickly zero in on the two primary gifts they owe their children: roots and wings. Roots ensure that the circumstances of life don't destabilize and debilitate them. Roots are their security, support, the home base of love. Wings will help children move forward in spite of obstacles, conquer their chal-lenges, and soar above their feelings of loss.

Dr. Dan Siegel, the bestselling co-author of *Parenting from the Inside Out* and several other parenting books and the executive di-rector of the Mindsight Institute, described what happens during a separation for the parents and for the children involved. "We are very relational beings," he explained. "We naturally form strong attach-ments to the people close to us, and this tendency begins at birth with an attachment to the person who gives us care most consis-tently. Often this is our mother, but it can be another person. The quality of this early attachment can vary, but in the most ideal circumstances, it provides a child with three things: the feeling of being Seen (physically, mentally, and spiritually), being Soothed (when you're distressed, your connection with this person is able to help calm you or make you feel comforted and at ease), being Safe (this person protects you). All these things lead to Security, and such an attachment gives a child a positive springboard into life."

Dr. Siegel goes on to explain that when we get older, our romantic partners become attachment figures—we seek to be seen, soothed, and safe in those relationships as well. Sometimes these adult relationships reflect the quality of our original attachments. Sometimes they act as a compensation for them. When there is a breakdown in that relationship, it is a deep rupture that has a huge impact on our lives. It is also a disruption for the children who bear witness to it.

During the early stages of my breakup, I was confused and experiencing great levels of emotional distress. I was numb. I woke up sad and went to sleep sadder. I didn't know where to start to find peace. While sadness enveloped me, my sweet boy was also sad. When I couldn't bear to peel myself out of bed to face the world, his innocent eyes looked concerned.

For the sake of my son's energy, I purged myself of the crying and screaming when he wasn't around and prayed before I was in his presence. It was important to not allow myself to pass down my stress into his little body. I knew how important it was to keep this child protected from the hazards of my own sadness. I remembered the four years I lived with my parents as I watched their twelve-year marriage rapidly devolve. One parent was constantly complaining about the other, and it was stressful. My sister and I internalized our parents' emotions and felt a little bit of what each parent felt for each other. I existed timidly in their presence, not sure where my own emotions fit into the picture. This was not a positive emotional experience for a child.

THE WAKE-UP CALL

I didn't want to involve Kasseem in my pain. My actions were all traits he could observe and silently absorb, and I knew that there was a distinct possibility that he might view my behavior and carry it into his adult life. I wanted him to be happy, and I began to understand that this would be unattainable without first finding my own happiness or, at the very least, a place of internal peace. I didn't want to mold his life in the negative radiation of my hurt.

Yet I wasn't masking what was happening very well. He began to ask questions about my relationship with his father. Kasseem is my little thinker. The family has coined him the King of Common Sense because he's always strategically working things out in his mind. He would wait until we were both alone and quiet before starting his inquiries about the life we were living. Many times he would wait until he was tucked into bed, or I would catch him staring into the rearview mirror, trying to make eye contact with me on our drives home from school.

"Mommy, does Daddy like you? Do you like him?"

During this time, visits with his father took place only every other weekend or whenever Swizz was in town. Kasseem noticed how Swizz and I barely smiled at each other during drop-off and pickup and how intense the energy was. Meeting to exchange Kasseem was just that—an exchange—like a FedEx guy scrambling to get a box out of his truck and running up the stairs to drop it at the front door. There were no emotions. No humanity. Kasseem wanted his parents to get along. He yearned for unity and harmony. There were more questions.

"Mommy, why doesn't Daddy ever come over to our house? And why can't you go to his house?"

These questions signaled that Kasseem was absorbing the negativity between his father and me. Instead of enjoying a carefree, innocent childhood, he was wrestling with very adult emotions. He began having a hard time at school. His teacher reported that he seemed to be having difficulty paying attention in class. He was very comfortable with his teacher at the time and told her that he didn't like having two homes and wished he had a normal family. He started to rebel in his own way.

Too often, parents hesitate to speak to their children openly about their separation. They mistakenly think, "If I ignore these questions, they will go away." Often parents are nervous about speaking to their child about what they have told themselves is their personal failure. Instead, they tell the child that everything will be fine. That may be true, but if we don't also affirm our children's feelings, we're doing a deep disservice to them.

Sophia Chang, a professional in the music business, knew that pretending to go along would not work: "Our children are bound to us in every way—spiritually, emotionally, physically, genetically. I don't care if both parents are Oscar-winning actors; you can never fool your kids into thinking that everything is okay. Even when the children are babies, they are so tuned in to our energy, they know something is amiss. When I told my mentor, Michael Ostin, about the challenges in my marriage—that we were fighting in front of the kids, that there was no joy, no tenderness between us—he said to me, 'Soph, is that really the model of love that you want for your children?' I knew he was right."

When Michelle Seelinger, a businesswoman and philanthropist, and her husband, David, decided to separate, she insisted that they tell their daughters together in the most loving, calm, and accepting atmosphere possible. They picked the family room of their home and struggled to find words that could convey that even though they loved each other and them very much, they needed to live in separate homes. The girls never had a clue anything was wrong with their parents, so it was very confusing to them. Their four-year-old didn't understand, but the eight-year-old was devastated. Michelle hadn't been too worried about their reactions, having been brought up seeing many broken families. But in that moment, she considered that in their affluent northern New Jersey community, most parents stayed together despite their problems. They would now be the only kids with a mom and a dad who don't live together or spend holidays or family vacations together. "I realized I had to step up and be strong for them if I was going to raise two young, confident, successful women all alone in a social media–obsessed society where normal was defined by Kardashian family values."

Adam, a married adult father of two children, remembers the exact day his father moved out of the house, even though he was only five years old. There had been a lot of arguing and yelling, and he figured something would have to change, but he wasn't sure what that change would look like until his father left. There was a degree of embarrassment. It was the early eighties, and divorce was very rare among his friends. He was also anxious about whether he and his brother would have to move to a different house. There was a perfunctory sit-down, during which his parents rolled out the common script: "Mommy and Daddy love you and your brother, but we need to live apart. This is not your fault." Now with children of his own, he wishes he was given an opportunity to learn more about what happened with his parents and describe what his concerns were at the time.

"How do I begin to discuss divorce and co-parenting with my child?"

World-renowned therapist and author Dr. Shefali Tsabary had important advice about this: "As parents, we cannot protect our child from feeling pain. This is their path. You must allow them to feel the pain, anger, and confusion that a separation inevitably causes. Your role is to be a witness to the pain, then help guide your child in the process of navigating that pain. Don't say to the child, 'Now, you're gonna get two families instead of one.' The kid didn't ask for two families. Be honest and transparent: 'We understand that you didn't ask for this. It is not your fault, and we are deeply sorry this is happening, but each person needs to find their own truth, and this is the way Mom and Dad are finding their truth.' It is important to help the child see that this is not the end of the world, that he or she is going to get through this. If the adults work to minimize conflict, minimize confusion, and minimize inconsistencies—which are the upshots of blending—the child will survive the process with dignity, confidence, and a sense of security."

Every parenting expert I spoke with emphasized the importance of being open with your child about your emotions and allowing him or her to give voice to feelings and fears during a breakup. Your child has developed a picture of normal in their mind. When there is something like a divorce, that picture shifts dramatically. It's confusing, and if they are not allowed to speak about it, then that confusion becomes internal and is magnified. They may begin to speculate on what they did to contribute to their parents' breakup. They may become cynical, sad, and/or angry people and grow up replaying feelings of abandonment with their future partners.

If you tell your child, "I'm okay," and you are quite clearly not okay, the message your child receives is "Don't trust your instincts. What you see and feel isn't true." The more productive route is to engage with your child in what Dr. Siegel describes as reflective dialogue. When things are calmer, you can sit with your child and gauge their reaction to what's happening. These conversations allow your child to be seen and soothed. Even when emotions bubble over with your ex right before your children's eyes, you can return to the incident and explain that adults in a state of anger or sadness do things that they wouldn't ordinarily do. You can help your child make sense of the situation.

Erica Reischer, author of *What Great Parents Do*, believes it's important to be open with your children: "Great parents acknowledge their moods and feelings." All kids, even very young ones, have "feelers." They know when their parents are sad or in a bad mood or, when a parent makes the well-intentioned mistake of hiding their feelings, are saying okay when clearly things are not okay. This is confusing for kids. When their feelings are not being matched with what the parent says, it is an incongruity that ultimately stunts their emotional intelligence.

At the same time, you should not overshare with your children. If your child is asking you why you are sad, you can say, "I'm sad because someone said something to hurt my feelings." That is easy for a child to understand. The language can become more sophisticated the older your child is, but there is no need to name the other parent. Sharing how you feel in a developmentally appropriate way will give you the opportunity to role model coping strategies for your child. Bashing your ex will compromise your relationship with your child, who will likely feel that you blocked the relationship with the other parent from developing. It may also cause your child to feel as if he or she needs to take care of you. At the end of the day, a child does not want to take care of his or her parent.

Children are remarkably resilient. I knew this to be true about Kasseem. However, that resilience needs to be guided. I had to think of a plan of action to produce change. I had to figure things out . . . quickly. Nothing in my life other than the love for my son could have forced me to rest my ego and pick up all the pieces of myself that I had lost along the way. My perspective needed to be broadened. The breakup was not what was happening to me; it's what was happening *for* me.

STARTING FROM THE BEGINNING

So where did I begin? How did I move forward from the sadness?

People always ask me this, and the answer is consistent—you first have to find the light in the dark places, and then create positives in areas once filled with the negatives. Moving forward has always been, and will always be, based on the achievement of peace within. There is no timeline for healing. The timing is and should be completely personal to the individual. I knew it was time to return to who I intended to be. So I started from my beginning.

My grandmother, who raised me, with Kasseem and me on his first birthday. I was pretty clueless when it came to a traditional family upbringing with a mother and a father under the same roof, but still I wanted that picture for my son more than anything.

When I was nine months old, I was brought to live with my grandmother, Philomene Tifrere. A spiritual and independent woman from the island of St. Lucia, her love, guidance, and powerful example made me the woman I am today. It was she, in fact, who taught me the importance of balance and owning my own identity. She gave me the tools that would soon help me see myself through my own healing and blending.

By the time I was born in 1978, she was fifty-four years old. She had birthed five children and seen five fathers leave. She had no idea what the inside of a courtroom looked like, and she certainly never saw a child-support check in her life. A scheduled visitation from one of her children's fathers would probably have seemed like a dream. Mum, as I call her, never used the term "single mother." She never claimed it. She just figured out how to be a mother on her own, while protecting her sanity and the well-being of her children.

Mum's love, guidance, and powerful example made me the woman I am today. It was she, in fact, who taught me the importance of balance and owning my own identity. She gave me the tools that would soon help me see myself through my own healing and blending.

Here I am in 1981 with Mum, holding my younger sister, Melissa. Mum was visiting us in Cambridge, MA.

Mum stood a gentle five feet, four inches and held a petite frame, but she spoke with the passion and conviction of a general leading an army of loyal warriors. She always wanted me to know that energy, good or bad, always passed. "Don't worry, it will pass, Mashonda, and God will never give us more than we can bite off," she would say. She flowed through life, and even when things were challenging, she never let her burdens become a part of her fabric. I don't recall ever witnessing Mum in a state of distress. She was consistent with her uplifting spirit and love, and this made me feel protected as a child. She also unmistakably understood that I was an individual with an independent soul rather than her possession, giving me the freedom to think for myself. I still feel the self-empowerment that was instilled in me by my grandmother during my formative years.

While racing into adulthood, it was tragically easy to misplace her lessons, creating a space left vacant for fear, guilt, blame, and myriad unanswered "why"s. Soon after the divorce, I retreated to the chilling cold of seclusion. The silence allowed reflection, which began to reawaken my dormant true self. I began to recall Mum's constant reminders that everything I would ever need was right inside me. I didn't need to seek myself in the hearts of others. I was equipped with every tool I needed to prosper.

HEALING PRACTICES

One of these tools was the act of mindful breathing. Mum taught me that whenever something hurts, take a deep breath.

Inhale.

Exhale slowly.

I didn't realize the power of breathing until I began to practice Pilates. I began to train five days a week for one hour. During Pilates, you cannot stop to think about anything outside of being on the mat, holding your core, and breathing. You do not have the energy to focus on anything outside the realm of that present moment. It was an escape from the other twenty-three hours that were so often a confused and emotional mess. Exercise in any form is a vital part of becoming and staying a healthy human, not only physically but mentally.

I began to take the magic of the breath outside the Pilates studio, conditioning my mind to believe that my past wasn't as real as my present. The good thing about the past is that we have the power to make it whatever we want it to be. I decided to use my past as a series of lessons, as moments in time that related to the journey of becoming who I was right then in that moment.

Choosing my thoughts and practicing Pilates helped me shift not only my mentality but also my body and brain. As my body developed into its best condition ever, my brain followed closely behind. I learned how to use breath to eliminate mental clutter, those things that prevented me from controlling my direction and focus.

The second step toward moving through the pain I was feeling was to take a deep look into myself. I used therapy to do it.

MIND EXPERTS

I've never been one of those people who placed a stigma on seeking psychotherapy. I actually always felt that the ones who sat on the receiving end of the couch and spilled their thoughts of fear, anger, and blame were the brave ones.

If you can pay a specialist to style your hair or paint your nails, why would you let your friends do those things? Same rule applies to therapy. Why talk exclusively to your friends about your issues and mental health when there are people who have studied human behavior and are trained to be professional, compassionate, objective, and knowledgeable?

Did I need therapy?

Well, nothing was normal about the way I had been feeling. I was struggling. There was a loss of motivation, and I felt overwhelmed. The question "Am I crazy?" went back and forth in my head. I decided to pray on it. I didn't know who to trust or who to ask about the matter. No one in my circle had ever had a therapy session. It's not a common thing in the African American community. Most of the women in my life moved through emotions without seeking professional assistance. They discussed them with peers who were too jaded by their own emotional layers to provide constructive feedback. I knew that wasn't the route I wanted to take with my healing.

I had met with a psychiatrist ten years prior, when I lost my son Angel. All it took was one session and I was able to gain a different perspective on the incident. Losing a baby is something I feel you never 100 percent get over, but that session helped me clear up 75 percent of the trauma. But this was different. I needed to be mentally stable for my son, and because of this, I was willing to take the first step and be completely open and vulnerable to a complete stranger.

What God presented to me was more than promising. I met Dr. Jeffrey Gardere on the set of *Good Day New York* as I was promoting the season premiere of *Love & Hip Hop*. He approached me and said, "Mashonda, I have been following your story. I want you to know that your family is going to rise from this." It was like we were meant to connect at that specific time. We scheduled a time to meet, and our first session turned into what is now an ongoing friendship.

As I drove to Dr. Jeff's home office in Harlem, I wondered about a number of things. Could I trust him? Would he judge me? To my surprise, he was more open and relatable than I'd ever imagined. I no longer felt as though I was sitting with a doctor; he made his humanity available to me. It allowed me to be comfortable and open up.

Dr. Jeff recognized that I was a very wounded woman presenting a front to the world. I so wanted to be that strong woman pushing through the hurt in order to be present for her son. He assured me that it was important to have that stiff upper lip for Kasseem's sake, that it was healthier for him if I could maintain dignity in my daily life. However, he also made it clear that I needed to heal and that my healing wasn't going to happen overnight. He warned me that I would sometimes wake up feeling great. Other times, I would feel absolutely terrible. It was a process, but he promised things would improve steadily.

Dr. Jeff invited me to use our sessions as a place to grieve the separation freely and fully. Talking about my feelings to someone I could truly trust lifted a lot of the pain and relieved large amounts of pressure. Pulling the emotions out of my brain and channeling them verbally was far healthier than drowning them in denial.

I met Terrie Williams, the woman who I now call my godmother, much later, in 2012. I walked out of a meeting, and there she was in the waiting room. Once again, how random. Our eyes met, and there was a magical connection. Terrie, a leader and advocate in the mental health field, was my first psychotherapist. She truly held my hand and my heart through it all. I felt Terrie's feminine spirit, and she took to mine. Our connection was similar to that of mother and daughter, which provided me with a very deep sense of love and security.

We traveled together, sat on park benches and couches together, cried together, and told each other how much we loved each other. Terrie showed me how to grow day by day. She gave me hope that I could and would experience an abundant life. She also knew I would one day publish my story and told me to never stop writing.

She was a source of protection that my soul needed and couldn't find anywhere else at the time. She didn't know anything about my life, so everything was fresh. As humans, sometimes it's important to experience the freshness that a new relationship carries, a new human interaction. Someone who can see you only in your present state, without all the attachments of your past. That's what I had with Terrie.

DEAR MASHONDA,
PLEASE FORGIVE MASHONDA

Emma Johnson, the author of *The Kickass Single Mom* and a popular blogger, made a valuable point about the period immediately after a breakup. You'll be angry—really angry—at the other person. This is okay. But you should ultimately realize that your feelings are rooted in anger at yourself. Perhaps you're mad at yourself for picking the wrong guy or for ignoring your goddess-given instincts. It's easy to play the victim, but just as it takes two people to have a successful relationship, it takes two people for a relationship to not work out. Forgive yourself for the choices you've made. Emma said, "If you forgive yourself, you can forgive him, and if you can forgive him, you can forgive yourself. Owning your part in the breakup is really difficult and takes time, but owning responsibility means taking back your power, which you will need to move forward."

Emma also advised that you be aware of the people who are around you. Those who truly love you might think supporting you or being on "your side" means they need to bash your ex. But you're never going to move forward if you surround yourself with negative messages. Instead, spend time with people who have overcome hardships where forgiveness was required.

I also think therapy is very helpful. Both Terrie Williams and Dr. Jeff helped me work through my emotions. The sessions weren't always easy: there were dreadful moments when going back into the past would instantly break me down. But there has to be a willingness to face these tough topics once they are identified.

Perhaps you've never considered sitting with a therapist. Perhaps, like me, you were unsure if a therapist was someone you could trust. Or you may think that rehashing the past is a waste of time, that you can get through this phase by just "being strong." In the immediate aftermath of a separation, I urge you to consider therapy, if only for three or four sessions.

A therapist can offer a fresh way of understanding the entire situation, which cuts a new path for the work you will do on your own. The sessions allow the opportunity to be vulnerable, which is important when you're working so hard to maintain a strong image for your children and the rest of the world. And, perhaps most important, therapy sessions get you in the practice of mental solitude, of taking time to retreat into the personal, intimate space that is your heart.

In his book *Parenting from the Inside Out*, Dr. Siegel speaks to the importance of a parent developing a coherent life narrative: "Coherence is a scientific word for when you reflect on the past, really be open to the positive and the negative incidents that have affected you, and then understand what you want to do about those to become the person you want to be."

In doing this self-work, you can free yourself up from the burdens of the past and be fully present for your child. Therapy was a way for me to reckon with my past, and that was certainly what happened. Remember the question that pressed my spirit after Kasseem was born: How do I begin to become the person I need to be for this soul I brought into the world? The answer was to reconcile with my past.

When a parent wrestles with their own emotional turmoil, it hinders the growth of the parent/child relationship. One must settle into a deep understanding of self in order to stand a chance at optimizing one's ability to attach and connect to their child. Being fully present for your child is especially vital during a divorce. To be present is to show up mentally and emotionally, prepared to offer empathy and comfort. That's nearly impossible if you're still swirling in confusion.

"Make sense of your life so that you can be present and show up for your child." —Dr. Dan Siegel

REBUILDING THE SPIRIT

Whether your relationship ended abruptly or was the result of a slow decline, the finality of a divorce or separation can be a severe rupture to the spirit if your expectations don't meet your relationship's final reality. It's like an earthquake. The ground you've been standing on moves, and the instability can tip you into making choices you wouldn't have otherwise made. Some of us fall into the cracks of sadness. Others patch ourselves up so that the world sees us as having it all together. The immediate task is to regain your composure, your peace. You have to get to the point where you accept your new normal. I had to withdraw from those things and those people who ignited my ego. I used the power of breathing to recenter myself in the present moment. I used exercise to release stress from my body, to have something to physically pull me out of self-conflict.

You have to find a way to heal the fracture; otherwise you won't have the energy or the foundation to do the deeper healing work needed to effectively co-parent. Every parent's goal is to have a child who thrives. Dr. Siegel explained the thriving child as one who has learned to know herself, has learned how to be compassionate and empathetic. The thriving child rises to challenges without collapsing and approaches life prepared to realize their full potential intellectually, emotionally, socially. If a parent is walking around broken, the energy will manifest negatively in the child. As parents, we can't afford to fall apart; our children's spirits and their sense of security are at risk.

GIFT YOURSELF

There is an insurmountable relief that comes with taking action to move in a different life direction. Seeking therapy was one of the most worthwhile gifts I could've ever given myself.

Gifting myself. That was one of the biggest corners I turned during this time in my life. Giving myself the gift of breath. Giving myself the gift of mental and physical exercise. Giving myself the gift of therapy.

I wasn't in the habit of being generous with Mashonda. I allowed the world around me to have too much control over my spiritual freedom, and I began to lose hope. I walked into a tattoo parlor and asked the artist to drill the seven-letter word "LOYALTY" into my hand. That tattoo was by far the most painful one of the ten I have. At the time, all I thought was, "You have to bring a new meaning to this word." I had been addicted to loyalty—loyalty to my husband and loyalty to my marriage. Once I began to rebuild my spirit, loyalty meant something new. It meant being at one with myself, loving Mashonda, and protecting her heart, soul, and energy first. That was one of the greatest lessons this whole experience taught me, and I share it now with you: Value yourself. Find a balance between loving yourself and loving others, but never sacrifice your worth. My tattoo now reminds me that loyalty starts within.

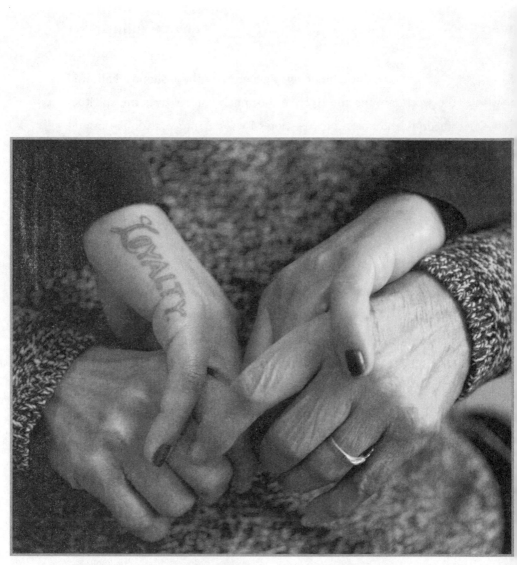

Value yourself. Find a balance between loving yourself and loving others, but never sacrifice your worth. Loyalty always starts within.

CHAPTER 3

Surrender

"Healing is the end of conflict with yourself."

—Stephanie Gailing

W hat do you want to be when you grow up?"

It's a question many ponder during their youth. Other common questions: Where will I live? Who will I marry? How many kids will we have? I asked myself all of these things. And the future was always optimistic: I was going to sing in front of audiences all over the world, I was going to meet the man of my dreams, have three kids, and live happily ever after.

Things didn't quite work out that way. When my divorce was final, all of a sudden I got hit with the "single mother" title. I saw women raising children on their own every day. My grandmother certainly did. But single motherhood simply wasn't a part of the plan. Or rather, it wasn't a part of *my* plan.

Whenever someone used the term "single mom," there was always a weird sense of deficiency attached to it. "I'm a single mom, so I have to work extra hard. I'm doing everything all alone." Or "I'm a single mom, so my child will have to figure many things out on his/her own, things I can't teach him/her." The truth is this: there is a tremendous amount of wholeness and richness in being a mother. No mother should ever feel diminished by society's labels.

As I said earlier, my grandmother never described herself as a single mom. She lived above any label, mostly by keeping God squarely on her side at all times. She would dismiss troubling situations by saying "I have to put it in God's hands." And she was a prayer warrior. With her eyes closed, she would slowly tilt back her head to look upward at the energy above her crown and begin a divine conversation. Or I would sometimes catch her lips moving at rapid speed on the subway or while she was doing housework. I believe she even prayed in her sleep. Prayer was how she released mental and emotional toxicity, the outlet she used to let go of her struggles. She replaced everyday drama and periods of confusion with words of gratitude directed toward God and the universe.

Mum and I attended church every Sunday. She was a prayer warrior, replacing everyday drama and periods of confusion with words of gratitude directed toward God and the universe. Witnessing the power of prayer from my grandmother was a part of my everyday life as a growing child. But in the luxury of my adult life, I forgot its magic.

Witnessing the power of prayer from my grandmother was a part of my everyday life as a growing child. But in the luxury of my adult life, I'd forgotten its magic. The hustle of the music industry made me believe that I needed to continuously fight to take control of my life. It was an exhausting and stressful way to live, but I didn't have a reason to change. If it weren't for my son and the need to become a great mother (and ultimately an evolved human), I probably wouldn't have realized the need to reconnect with a higher power. I had to relearn faith and surrender in order to live a truly optimal life.

THE SECRET OF LETTING GO

My first step on this journey toward my reeducation wasn't one I sought out. A friend who had become tired of hearing me victimize myself, blame others for my unhappiness, and hold on to the security blanket of suffering gave me a book by Guy Finley called *The Secret of Letting Go.* I accepted the gift with weariness. My ego already (falsely) insisted that I revel in self-pity and look for the easy way out of this labyrinth of pain I had created around myself. I couldn't foresee how a collection of words could alter my entire outlook.

When I picked up the 312-page softcover book, I was both fatigued and curious. Fatigued because I had already searched outwardly for the answers. I traveled. I shopped. I partied. I dated. Nothing had worked. My failed marriage still weighed heavily on me. The description on the back cover of the book promised a way out of this unhappiness. I was curious to find out how to let go of the thoughts and ideas I'd created in my mind about what my life and family should look like.

Pay attention to how you feel the next time something doesn't go your way. Does your energy shift? Does your vibe drop down to a lower frequency, and you immediately feel some level of discouragement? Even if for only a second, it is guaranteed that one of these reactions will come to the surface. Having these human feelings isn't the issue. We all start off with a wish list of expectations and plans, and we often cling to these ideals so dearly that there's no room for a different take. The problem arises when a person is unable to identify these emotions and move forward from them. How long does it take you to let go of this feeling of frustration? How long does it take for you to move forward?

Early in our breakup, people who were far away from the situation, perched behind glowing computer screens, would write, "You need to give it up, it's over" and "Move on!" They passed judgment on my life and decisions, and it was hurtful. Tons of unsolicited, unhelpful advice and not one person used the "S" word. No one told me it was okay to surrender.

Guy Finley's book changed my perspective on the art of surrender and the magic of releasing negative thoughts forever. The full meaning of the word "surrender" is rarely expressed in our culture. People look at the word "surrender" and immediately associate it with weakness. We think surrender is simply giving up. Now, I recognize it takes tremendous courage to wave the white flag; there are extraordinary layers of beauty in giving up. When you give up on the things and people who don't serve your higher purpose, you are better able to accept the unlimited blessings waiting to pour down on you. Everyone and everything enters our lives in order to teach us a lesson. It's up to us to absorb the lesson. That's the whole reason why we experience pain: it's a reminder to absorb and remember the lesson. This is all a part of our evolution.

I read the book at least eight times. I studied it. I wanted to retain the information and quickly apply it to my own life. During this exercise, I began to notice how much of my pain came with holding on to hurtful things—ideas, memories, thoughts, circumstances. I started to release all of what I thought I was supposed to be (a wife in a traditional family) and was slowly able to remove myself from blocking my own path. With practice and conscious efforts, I stopped blaming my ex-husband for my unhappiness. For the first time, I understood that resistance blocks a person from fully evolving from their life experiences. I began to let God flow through me.

The Secret of Letting Go gave me a new and refreshing paradigm. I wanted to get out of that rut—that constant state of suffering—for good. I made a decision to begin the most challenging work I would ever encounter: self-work. Mental health is what truly sustains us as human beings. No matter how strong one pretends to be, mental and emotional wounds take the longest time to heal. The wounds can and will reopen throughout a lifetime if they are not properly treated and cared for.

Knowing how to begin was the first step to conquering the overall battle. Healing from any life-altering experience, be it physical or emotional, must take place in stages of self-awareness and self-care. It requires discipline. I had to remind myself each day why I needed to change. I had to form a steady relationship with the person I wanted to be, my higher self, the version of me that embodied love and spread light. To be able to simply focus on being a positive person, you must be willing to tear yourself to pieces, sort through it all, collect the parts that you love, and dispose of the pieces you don't need. That's the debris that will only feed your ego.

The alternative to healing is regret. Granny Sandra helped me realize that divorce or the end of a relationship is hard, but one must accept it. Moving on is key, especially when you have children. In her infinite mother-wit, Granny Sandra reminds us, "As difficult as it may be, set aside your personal hurt. Get up and improve yourself instead of holding on to the pain. The love you have for your children can be your motivation. Their happiness and peace of mind comes first."

These were my steps to healing.

IDENTIFY THE PAIN

When something physically hurts, our natural instinct is to find out where on the body we've been hurt and what caused the injury. This also applies to mental anguish. What is hurting, and what has caused the pain? Is it a familiar feeling?

At first it was hard to tell what was truly hurting me. My mind was always spinning, and I wasn't present in my current state. Before I moved out of the home I shared with my ex-husband, I opened up to our neighbor, who was a dedicated father and husband. I asked him if the pain I felt from the separation was normal. He said, "Yes, if the heart is fully involved." He advised me to stop running from my feelings, that I needed to write down all the words that described what I was feeling so that I could immediately work on fixing them. There were two words that surfaced immediately.

Lonely—I felt like a lost, unloved child with no mother, no father, no one to care for me.

Unworthy—I placed a lot of blame on myself. What could I have done better for my husband? I felt I didn't look good enough, that my career didn't match up to his. I worried so much that Kasseem Jr. would one day question my ability to be a wife. "Why didn't you and Daddy make it work for our family?"

These thoughts had been eating away at me. Identifying these thoughts clearly was the first essential step to purging them.

FOCUS ON LOVE

An important part of the healing process is returning to the things you love: your passions and talents. I stopped writing songs the way I once did. I still sang, but it wasn't from my heart anymore. The talents that God had given me were withering away, much like eyes that refuse to stay open ultimately lose sight. Sometimes when women focus so much on supporting their partners and their children, they end up feeling as though they don't having anything left for themselves. After a divorce or breakup, it is important to quickly regain your own identity.

When I woke up to myself after a year of solitude, I was determined to regain my identity as Mashonda the human, the artist, and the woman. I didn't want to simply be "Swizz's ex" for the rest of my life. I never wanted Kasseem to one day google my name and see only a bunch of media trash. Getting out of the "ex-wife" box meant no more public stunts of emotional brokenness, no more gossipy interviews, no more extra-sensitive social media posts, and, most of all, a very private, personal life. I realized that the less negativity I gave onlookers to talk about, the quicker they would stop associating me with my divorce.

I realigned with what felt good, putting an end to the feelings that were stunting my growth. Following my grandmother's example, I reprogrammed my mind to be optimistic and hopeful no matter what life was throwing my way.

I wanted my son to witness me pushing to become the best version of myself no matter the circumstance. I set up some ambitious goals, and the more I worked toward them, the more I felt whole. With every self-help book and every writer's workshop that I sat in on, I regained and refined pieces of myself that were stolen by ego. I was falling in love with myself all over again. The weight I was carrying began to get lighter. Love is the most powerful force in the universe, and this belief gave me permission to be vulnerable and honest with myself and others.

AWARENESS

During therapy, I learned the universal rules that are attached to emotions, unconscious triggers, blame, and forgiveness. Being able to tap into your emotions is one thing. Allowing them to rule and define you is another. I used to confuse emotions with feelings, not knowing how different they really are. Emotions are born from past experiences. They lay dormant in your unconscious mind until they are triggered by conscious thoughts. At any moment, an internal or external event can take place and trigger an emotion that will then lead to a feeling. Whether the feeling is good or bad all depends on how we are willing to perceive and accept it.

Terrie Williams really helped me process how to recognize an emotional trigger. "Somebody says something to you, somebody does something to you, and there is a shot of pain. You don't necessarily know what happened to affect you so deeply. Or there may be something that when you even begin to speak about it, the tears start to flow. Just speaking something out loud reveals how unresolved the underlying emotional issue is," she told me.

Before doing the inner work necessary to identify my negative triggers (behavioral responses to past events), I was constantly blaming everyone for my life troubles. I had to reverse this energy onto myself and then determine the true origin of my issues. I learned that my parents' divorce was one of the triggers that followed me through life. Talking to my grandmother, mother, and father about their divorce was very helpful in letting go of all the awful things I had stored in my mind about a family ending.

You see, I came from three generations of women who had accepted abandonment as a sorrow owed to them. I remembered my grandmother's sadness when she described her childhood. Her father was a French fisherman who impregnated an island girl (my great-grandmother) and simply moved on to another port. Mum only knew her father when he decided to show up in her life. And even though he showed up often, she always yearned for more of his love and fatherly affection.

She, in turn, gave birth to my father on the island of Barbados when she was twenty years old. His father turned his back on them immediately, and that experience changed the way Mum viewed men forever. She never let go of that pain. She went on to have four more children but wouldn't allow herself to trust a man fully again.

I was bathed in this history, so it's no surprise that as a child and as a young adult, I had such a deep yearning for a traditional family. I would always say, "I never want my family to split up like that. I never want to have to separate my family the way my parents did." When it happened to me, it was my ultimate fear incarnated. It was a reason for me to look down on myself. This awareness gave me an opportunity to release the negative bias that came with this trigger.

What happened to my grandmother was unfortunate. But my situation was entirely different. Even though my marriage had ended, Swizz would never turn his back on his child, would never be absent from Kasseem's life. This I knew in my core. With that assurance, I could broaden my perception. Divorce wasn't a precursor to abandonment. I had to shift the meaning of divorce from what I knew as a child it to be (fear and shame) to what I would ultimately accept and embrace it to be as a woman—a rebirth, an opportunity to live a new life.

This clarity brought me closure from unhealed wounds I'd been carrying for my whole life. And it helped me let go of the blame I had piled onto Swizz and Alicia. This choice was paramount in my healing process. All blame had to disappear.

Blame devolves the spirit. There is never a reason to blame anyone for anything. No one has the power to hurt you. You are the only person who has that ability, and you are the only person who has the power to truly make yourself happy.

My sanity meant more to me than continuing to play the victim in a corny horror movie. I have gotten to the point where I see life for exactly what it is: a series of lessons lived out through encounters and experiences, with the end goal being human evolution.

Rather than drown in your own misery, you owe it to yourself to do the work and move forward.

CRY-CLEAN-BANDAGE

Once I was able to pinpoint my pain, I spent some time in tears. I cried a lot, some days more than others. I never felt ashamed of crying. My soul needed the release. When I cry, I feel the most open, the most vulnerable. When I allow myself to weep, I forget how to breathe; I am forced to surrender—to hand my life over to my Creator. Time slows down, and life feels timeless. I forget where I am, and I allow myself, without resistance, to connect all the pieces of me that are falling apart.

Crying activates the opportunity to rebuild.

Tears have the power to cleanse negative physical effects on the body. Immediately after crying you feel a reduced amount of emotional stress. At first it's okay to acknowledge hurtful feelings but you don't want to nurture them for too long. Quickly release them. You have to move on to cleaning up what are really self-inflicted wounds. Shift your emotions by purging all forms of negativity. The ego—my false self—fought against this. It wasn't who I was that was holding me back. It was who I thought I was, who I thought I would be without a man.

I began to talk to my ego.

"Remove your hands from over my eyes so that I may see the real beauty of the world. Unplug my ears so that I can hear the truth. Get out of my head so that I can have space for my freedom."

I realized that no one but me had control over my thoughts. I was the ruler of my mind. I had been giving away my power for too long by putting my energy into the wrong things and looking for validation in the wrong places. I had to take a full step toward purging and detoxing myself from all forms of negativity. I cleaned up my thoughts. I shifted my emotions.

And then came the bandages. After you cry, after you properly clean a wound, you have to wrap it all up carefully and reengage with life.

People say that time heals all things, but keep in mind that time is not the healer—you are. When it comes to recovery, you must do the self-work, raise the white flag, so that God can work out everything that is not in your control. And then let divine timing take over.

When a child has a bandaged wound, they will often peek under the bandage to check for blood or signs that their skin is healing. They will pick and pull on the scab, hoping that it will make the boo-boo go away faster. Of course this action only prolongs the healing process. As parents we know this, so we ask them not to interfere with the bandage. But are we practicing what we've preached to our young learners when it comes to our own healing? Anxious healing will never have a successful outcome. You must leave yourself alone. The less you interfere with your wound, the faster it will heal and the smoother the scar will be.

While the bandage is on the wound, take good care of yourself. Seek out the things that bring you joy. Continue to train your mind to think positively.

Sometimes a child will be so busy playing that they forget they have the bandage on. By the time they've noticed the protective shield has fallen off, the injury has already healed. The same thing happens to adults in the process of emotional healing.

And that was my experience.

One chilly November morning in 2011, the brisk air on the back of my neck awakened me. The sunlight bled through the curtains. I emerged from underneath my down comforter, and when I sat up, it felt as if gravity had departed. Everything seemed new. On that glorious morning I removed my bandage and stepped out of my bed into a freedom that had been missing for years.

I breathed deeper.

I smiled easier.

I became one with myself again.

And I was ready to take the first step at making things right with my co-parents.

CHAPTER 4

Honor Thy Co-Parent

'd been living on my own for almost two years, and there was an undeniable feeling of independence that came with that. For the first time in my life I was in charge of paying all the bills, getting oil changes on my car, and trying to figure out what kind of insurance I should purchase for my home. I was thirty-one years old and had no idea how any of this stuff worked because Swizz always took care of these things.

I had stepped into grown-woman-handle-your-business land, and there was no turning back. In the beginning, being in charge of every aspect of my life was scary. But slowly it became very liberating and served as further proof that I had been living too small, in a comfort zone where I had been too dependent on my husband. I hadn't given myself a chance to explore my own potential. There's nothing wrong with allowing a man to be a provider, but as women and mothers, we have to constantly empower ourselves to be self-sufficient and absolute in our own identity. It is important to invest in yourself, further your education, and follow through with your dreams and goals.

When I parted ways with Swizz, I was unsure as to how I would start my life over. I knew I had a few things to fall back on—writing, art, music—but it took some time for me to move forward on these things because I was so consumed by the divorce. Once I began on this new journey of independence, the energy around me kept sending signs to remind me that I was meant to be more, learn more, and do more. All I had to do was gracefully pursue it.

Throughout your entire blending experience, it is important for your child to witness you living a full, magnificent life. Being proactive and purpose-driven helps instill the value of independence in your child and removes attention from the actual demise of the relationship.

THE BIGGER PICTURE

I had completed most of the self-work. A large portion of my wounds had been healed, and I had started a very private love affair with this really amazing woman named Mashonda. This one-on-one romance made me realize my blessings. Finally I knew that everything happened the way it was supposed to. My perspective broadened, and like an eagle flying high above, I had access to a panoramic view of my life. The events of my past were all designed to teach me how to be a more powerful human being, a wiser woman, and a more present-minded mother. I saw things for what they were, why they had happened, and how I ultimately wanted them to be. With this belief and mentality, everything and everyone around me was now filtered through the lens of love and light. And I realized that Swizz wasn't my enemy. He wasn't a monster. In fact, he was one of my biggest blessings, because he gave me the greatest love of my life, Kasseem Jr.

"Why should I bother making amends with my ex? My ex and I can't stand each other, and the less we communicate, the less strife. And his new partner has nothing to do with my life!"

For many years I've heard people, both mothers and fathers, say that they don't have any desire to become friends with their co-parent or get to know the co-parent's new significant other. Their reasons: they don't like them, and they don't trust them.

I understand all these reasons, and I know that it's not easy to let go of the feelings that come with being hurt or disappointed. But I can tell you this: resentment, hate, and blame are characteristics that your child will always identify with you. They will never forget the way their parents handled situations when they were young. Use yourself as an example. I'm sure that you have memories from your childhood of the adults closest to you acting out. How did it make you feel then? How does it make you feel now?

Not everyone prioritizes their human evolution; some are content with living at a low frequency. Those of us who want better for ourselves and our children, who want a healthy, stress-free parenting experience, will work to heal the rift in some capacity. Even if it's just to the point of being able to hold a decent conversation about your child. You don't want to wake up one day a grandmother still holding on to the same fears and negative emotions. Or maybe you do, but that's none of my business.

Ultimately, the need to raise my son to manhood with the help of his father trumped my need to be melancholic and angry.

Life has proven over and over again that it's impossible to practice love and hate in the same breath. After the divorce, Swizz and I despised each other. Our very public separation had charged our egos. For years all we did was argue. We argued with each other in front of judges and surrounded by our family. We had forgotten what each other's souls looked like and became strangers, no longer recognizing each other's humanity. And, like many newly separated or divorced parents, there was no harmony or balance between us. Truth is, I didn't hate Swizz, and he didn't hate me. We were just both stuck in remnants of the toxic clutter that occupied our minds during the divorce.

Once I began to heal my wounds of anger and confusion, I knew hanging on to negative feelings about Swizz would not serve me well or uplift my situation. I refused to be remembered as a mother who was bitter, unfit, or set on telling everyone how much she couldn't stand her child's father. I began to reassess all that Swizz had provided me—the fun times and the challenges. I remembered all the great experiences we shared as young adults—from recording music in a small-bathroom-turned-vocal-booth in a Harlem apartment, to sleeping on the hardwood floor in our first rental all winter because we couldn't afford furniture. We went through a lot, always with gratitude, always believing things would only keep getting better. By doing this I recognized that what I thought I lost was minuscule compared to what I had gained.

According to world-renowned therapist and author Dr. Shefali Tsabary, there is a soul contract between intimate partners. Too often we're focused on a "romantic" ideal of possessing or owning someone's heart and affection forever. However, the contract between partners is not immutable. It is constantly shifting and transforming, because as individuals we consistently shift and transform. It's actually quite challenging to remain on the same evolutionary pace as your spouse. This explains why there is such a high divorce rate.

Dr. Shefali encourages us to think about divorce differently. Intimate relationships are here to guide us toward personal development. We need to ask ourselves, "What do I need to learn from this intimate partner?" Instead of labeling separation as a failure, we can simply understand that two people came together, learned what they needed to learn from each other, and have now shifted to a new phase of life. It's difficult for the ego to accept this, especially in the middle of heartbreak. But the peace this realization will bring to you creates the space for cooperation between former partners.

If you are steeped in unresolved conflict with your ex, your child's emotional balance will be thrown off. Children, being unable to understand the complexities of adult relationships, often take a divorce personally and may feel guilty about it. But if the parents are able to keep their own emotions at bay, managing the feelings of loneliness, depression, and/or anxiety that have come to the surface, their children will make it through this transition with less negative impact.

A DIFFERENT TYPE OF LOVE

If a desire for your ex lingers, you cannot blend. You have to learn how to accept a simple truth: the ex, once a romantic partner, is not yours anymore. The dynamic has changed. You can't hang on to old feelings and wants. You must release the past and focus on your new life with your child. This is why self-healing is a key first step to blending. It enables you to fully let go of the romantic relationship. If your heart is still tugged by your ex romantically, if you still have a desire for that type of love with this person, then you are not ready for blending.

In my case, Swizz was the father to our son, the other half of Kasseem's DNA, my partner in parenting. Nothing more. I was aware that our season had passed, and our reason for meeting and being together all those years had manifested in delivering an amazing child to the world.

However, once you release the relationship from romantic expectations, the feeling that remains cannot be indifference. As my son's other half, there was no way that I could make his father less significant than he was. One must connect with one's ex on a deeper level in order to blend effectively.

The ancient Greeks identified different types of love. There is *Eros*, love of the body, which is a passionate, romantic, and sexual connection. There is *Philia*, love of the mind, or brotherly love shared between friends based on shared values. *Storge* is the love between a parent and a child, and there is also *Agape*, the love of the soul, which is unconditional, compassionate, without an expectation of it being returned. My love for Swizz falls somewhere between *Philia* and *Agape*. I accept him as he is, selflessly and unconditionally, without expectations. There is nothing he can do or say to me personally to change the way I love him as a parenting partner to our son. I accept him for who he is in my life, and we have a familial connection.

Perhaps you can't imagine ever being at the point of *Agape* or *Philia* with your ex. That's understandable. Ego has a way of painting over the things that really matter, like love, empathy, and compassion, disguising them so that they're hard to locate. Usually, if all you're doing is arguing with a person you were once close to, it's because you've fallen out of alignment with the reasons why you once loved them. Our children have the power to help us restore the love we once had for the other parent. For me, the memory of Swizz placing our newborn son in front of my face provides that magic. This small person had just left my body and was placed in his father's arms even before I saw him. When Swizz introduced me to Kasseem that morning on the operating table, he cemented our bond as a family. How could I just push that moment out of my memory bank?

Everyone has at least one reason or one memory, whether it be big or small, that can be the root from which love and understanding can grow. Even if you don't have a past relationship with your co-parent, you have what is right before your eyes: the beautiful fact that together you've brought a child into the world.

THE PARENT CONTRACT

There was one very important thing we would always share: unconditional, nonjudgmental, and everlasting love for Kasseem. I knew for sure that Swizz wanted to be a great father. This was honorable and needed to be the guiding principle in all our interactions with each other.

Kasseem had a parenting contract with both me and his father. It was important for Kasseem's development that Swizz be allowed to fulfill the terms of this unspoken, divine contract.

There is one very important thing Swizz and I will always share: unconditional, nonjudgmental, and everlasting love for our son.

I believe that children choose their parents. Their souls come prepared to teach us what we need to learn in order to evolve as people. In the moment that you decide to carry a fetus full term or consciously take responsibility for a life that you may not have birthed, you open yourself up to a new realm of connectivity and love. You've taken a divine oath with Mother Nature, God, and the universe, a pledge to do your best as the caretaker of that child.

Dr. Shefali Tsabary describes this contract so beautifully: "As parents we must realize that our children are not born to meet our expectations. This understanding is born from ego-dominant thinking. In fact, the parent contract strikes at a deeper, more complex level where two beings relate to each other on a soul level. Both parent and child are here to help each other uncover their most true selves. Children are actually capable of teaching their parents more than their parents can ever teach them."

In the heated moments between couples, some mothers will keep their children from their fathers because they aren't getting what they want. Putting an innocent spirit in the line of fire because of your own selfish needs is a reckless game. Later in your child's life, you will likely be stuck trying to explain why you decided to stunt the growth of one of the most important relationships your child will ever know.

I knew that denying my son's father access to him was taking away my son's rights, more so than his father's. Kasseem had a parenting contract with both me and his father. It was important for Kasseem's development that Swizz be allowed to fulfill the terms of this unspoken, divine contract. Therefore, I never used my son as a pawn to get my own way, not even in my deepest moments of anger and pain. Such behavior would interfere with the invisible but very dominant parenting contract. And it's not worth it.

I knew that, even if I'd wanted to, I could not handicap Kasseem's relationship with Swizz in any way. I love my grandmother with everything that I am. She was a superb caretaker. However, the fact that I didn't develop a full bond with either my mother or my father left an open space in my spirit. I didn't want Kasseem to suffer with this lack the way that I did. For me, being the best mother I could be to Kasseem meant that I should encourage his relationship with his father. Ultimately, I was not responsible for their relationship—it would be what Swizz and Kasseem made of it—but I could have a hope for it. And I did. I knew that if Swizz and I could truly work together, so that we could both be fully in Kasseem's life, this would improve our son's chances at becoming a highly resilient and emotionally connected adult.

The other blending mothers I spoke to agreed wholeheartedly. Sheree didn't mince words on the topic. When it comes to mothers withholding their children from their fathers, she said, "Shame on them!" To her mind, probably the cruelest thing you can do to your child is to prevent them from seeing their other parent. She sees it as a slow destruction to a child's spirit. "If your child isn't in danger physically or emotionally, then your decision to withhold your child from seeing him as a power play is actually you deciding that revenge or bitterness is more important than the love you have for your child."

According to Emma Johnson, there are more than fifty peer-reviewed studies that prove that shared parenting is best for children. When children spend at least 40 percent of their time with each parent, it allows for real relationships. Fathers who see their child only four times a month are visitors, not parents with responsibilities. Emma believes this type of marginalization of dads—men who seem like nothing more than a paycheck to their children—is at the root of fatherlessness in this country.

I spoke to Malik Yoba, an actor, activist, and the proud father of three children, about his experiences after the separation from his first daughter's mother, and he told me, "I think a lot of times, people don't realize the connection that men have to their children. They think that because we don't carry [our children], we don't have the same connection. But for those of us who really are about the relationship, the connection is as deep as if we gave birth to them ourselves. I was in the family birthing center. I delivered my daughter, literally pulling her out into the world. I cut the umbilical cord. I named her. I would never want to be prevented from being with her."

The vast majority of fathers want to have their own time with their children, want to be actively involved. Swizz was and is certainly one of those fathers. And our son Kasseem deserved to witness unconditional love and partnership within his own family experience.

> **"Often the strife between parents after they've split is over money. I think a woman is totally within her rights to keep her child away from the father if he's not respecting his financial obligations."**
>
> This is wrong. In moments like this, we must think long term. Who are we truly hurting here? It's not the adult; it's the child. Children aren't thinking about money. They yearn for connection and love. As mothers, we must never take that away from them.
>
> Now, don't get me wrong. As parents, we are caretakers, and there is no getting out of financial responsibility. Sophia Chang said: "Don't ever hope that the father will contribute, and if he does, it's gravy, but you're the meat." Ultimately, your parenting contract and your financial obligations are two different things and should be kept in completely separate compartments. You should not feel as though a visit with a parent is like feeding a parking meter.

COURAGEOUS CONVERSATIONS

The first step Swizz and I took to rebuild our relationship was communication. After our breakup, we hadn't really talked about anything real, about true matters of the heart.

One of my favorite Jay-Z quotes is "You can't heal what you don't reveal." This is true. Swizz and I both had our hearts set in certain places, and for us to unite, we needed to hear and understand each other's voices. We had never developed a habit of discussing our issues, and so lots of hurt and pain existed beneath the surface. One hundred questions and unsolved mysteries surrounding our breakup lay heavily on my heart. In order to forge a new relationship based on the friendship we had before we were married, Swizz and I needed to wipe the slate clean.

I prepared myself to be vulnerable. In matters that deserve a fair chance of change, one must be brave enough to be human, to remove the mask, and to bear the soul. I wasn't going into the conversation as "tough Mashonda." As a gift to myself, I became the Mashonda who wanted to understand and who was willing to present a window of vulnerability in order to be understood.

I also adjusted my frame of mind. I shifted and cracked open the little square box of thinking patterns that I was living in, making room to live beyond the theories and thoughts that I had cultivated over the years about my breakup. I wouldn't allow myself to be negatively affected by anything Swizz might say; this conversation was not going to turn into an argument. My guard was down; my ego was in check. I had done enough self-work prior to our conversation and was feeling like a sensei, a master of self. I knew that my openness was coming from a place of love, and I was prepared to disagree gracefully with whatever didn't strike me as supportive of my own truth.

We can be so invested in our own truth that we're willing to kill any chance of peace to keep our personal truth alive. This way of thinking hinders human development. In order for us to evolve, we need duality, differences, and diverse opinions. That opinion may feel like a lie to the person hearing it, but you can condition yourself to not respond reactively. You can control what you say or do to make the situation better. Taking a battle stance will likely only make things worse. Swizz had his own perspective, and that needed to be respected in order for there to be neutrality. There's no button one can push to make people see things our way. We are all living and breathing different lives. Ultimately, I knew that one thing was for sure, and it was that moving forward, this couldn't be about my feelings anymore. This was about our son and his present and future well-being.

I was standing next to my dining room table when I typed into my cell phone, "Are you free to talk?" Just before I hit send, there was a little anxiety. Ego rose up, and I felt resistance. But I quickly checked myself and returned to the vision board I'd created in my mind of a healthy son and a fearless mother. Swizz replied yes, and I called right away, immediately laying all my cards on the table. I expressed my deep concern for our son's emotional well-being. Swizz was also concerned for our son. We both wanted Kasseem to feel comfortable in his own skin. We wanted him to be happy and free, to be able to love everyone and genuinely express that feeling without being afraid.

This common ground was the foundation for a far-reaching conversation. I asked him everything I had ever wanted to know, all the things that had eaten away at me for the past several years, all my doubts and fears. He realized my questions deserved honest answers and explanations. And in that first forty-five-minute conversation, he faced them head on. His answers were as detailed as he could make them. I didn't agree with everything he said. But it was his truth, and it was just as valid as mine.

I'm grateful that we opened up and began clearing the air in that first phone call. We were being vulnerable with each other, and it was working. Kasseem was our biggest responsibility, and we weren't going to let our pride or ego put our son at risk. We had to fix this. We committed to continue talking and building a new relationship. Each time we spoke after these phone calls, our communication got easier and smoother. We were nicer to each other, and this was a practice that needed to become a lifestyle, because our son was paying attention.

THE NEW WAY FORWARD

We spent hours on the phone digging deep and cleaning up our thoughts. We listened to each other and gave each other a chance to speak without yelling or getting upset. No one won and no one lost in these conversations. We found a weird place for a new friendship rooted in mutual respect and honesty. Eventually we'd return to the feeling of true family.

Were our conversations easy? No. Could they have happened if I hadn't done the self-work, if I hadn't let go of what I thought my life would be? Not at all. Can I say that our efforts were worth it? Absolutely. The evolved conversations that we shared during this time enabled us to return to a safe place in our relationship, forming a new, more solid foundation than the one before.

Swizz and I didn't have everything figured out overnight, but it didn't take us long to know that we had to put our best foot forward for Kasseem. We started to do nice things for each other, even when we really didn't want to. Every birthday or Christmas, we always made sure that Kasseem was involved in exchanging presents from one parent to the other. We faked the funk seamlessly for many years until it was sincere.

I specifically remember my thirty-fourth birthday, when Swizz did one of the kindest things for me that he had done in years. He told me to meet him and Kasseem outside Cipriani's, a restaurant downtown, on West Broadway. They pulled up in a black SUV and out jumped my little man, all suited up and ready to celebrate his mom. Kasseem grabbed my hand and walked me in the door with a smile on his face. He was so proud to be taking his mom out for her birthday. Swizz left his credit card with the waiter and told me to order whatever I wanted. Kasseem was experiencing something he and every child deserves to witness—humanity between his parents. The dinner ended with a chocolate cake and smiles that would never be forgotten. I believe Swizz felt I deserved a nice birthday, but did he do it for only my pleasure? No. In fact, we were in the middle of resolving some lingering legal issues stemming from our divorce. But regardless of that, Swizz intentionally gave his son a memory, downloading love and compassion into his young mind. And that in itself was a great pleasure for me, a more important gift than anything I could ever unwrap.

A PLAN COMING TOGETHER

My vision for a healthy future for my son and myself started to fall in place. The initial steps were clear and complete:

1. I had to purge myself of pain and hurt and reconnect with my higher self.
2. I had to create a safe platform for open communication with Swizz.

The final step to truly blending was starting a relationship with Swizz's wife. I had a relationship with all of Kasseem's school teachers and his babysitters. Even his physician gave me permission to always call if I had any questions. I wanted to have that same openness and availability with his new caretaker, his bonus mom. Blending doesn't exist if all parties are not on one accord and in constant communication with one another. As two mothers, we would become the two strongest forces in the equation. The relationship went to the very dynamic of womanhood, feminine energy, and resilience.

CHAPTER 5

A Letter from a Father

by Swizz Beatz

O n October 9, 2016, my wife had a huge concert in Times Square. Mashonda was invited and showed up. There was a rap artist backstage who took me aside and said, "Man, how did you do this?" "How'd I do what?" I replied. "The two women. In the same room." His face looked like he was seeing magic. He's not the first guy to react this way to our family.

Many people will be able to relate to our story, and working through the steps Mashonda outlines in this book can help anyone—men and women both—to reframe their co-parenting relationships. Mashonda asked me to write a chapter from my perspective as a father, and I was happy to do it.

To answer the question "How'd you do it?," I'd first have to say that I didn't do anything alone. All three of us—Mashonda, Alicia, and I—played a vital part. To understand my way into the solution, I'd have to help you understand how I look at being a father.

THE COACHES

I was fortunate to have three father figures in my life. Each one gave me a window into manhood, into fatherhood.

I'd have to start with my great-grandfather Bubba Dean. I lived with him and my great-grandmother Mable Dean in the early part of my life. He and I had a special bond. We used to have what he called "man-to-man talk." I was young—maybe about five, maybe even younger—and he'd say, "Come on. Before you go to bed, let's have man-to-man talk." He'd come into my room with a plate of fried fish, some hot sauce, and a can of Olde English 800, and he'd ask me about my day. I had the freedom to say whatever was on my mind—no censorship. It was a chance to air out my frustrations. And no-body could interrupt us. He and my great-grandmother were a tight team, but if she came into the room, he'd tell her we were having man-to-man talk and she'd back her way out. That time was just between him and me. And I loved it. Mostly because I usually ended up getting a toy or a pair of shoes or something. Now I realize that he was teaching me how to talk through things, how to be vocal. It was how I learned to communicate—skills that I pull on every day as an adult. And knowing my great-grandfather saw me as a little man helped me recognize the man I would become.

Bubba Dean drew a lot of respect from people. He was like the mayor in our Bronx neighborhood, like a diplomat. If folks had any problems, they'd come to my great-grandfather and he'd fix them. Your bike was stolen? He'd get it back. He and my great-grandmother ran the tenants' patrol. They maintained order in the building. Mrs. Lily might have some groceries to take upstairs, and the tenants' patrol would stop a young man and ask him to help her upstairs with her bags. It didn't matter where you were on your way to; you'd stop to help Mrs. Lily out of respect. If there was a mess in the hallway of your floor, either my Bubba or Mable would hand a broom and trash bag to the kids who lived on that floor. Boom, that floor was cleaned up, no problem.

One time this teenager, Hector, threw my shoe over the fence, and I told my great-grandfather about it. "Why'd he throw the shoe I worked hard to buy over a fence?" he asked me. And I explained that I was playing in the park, and they didn't want kids in the park. It wasn't even a big deal to me, but Bubba wasn't going to let that slide. He had me point out Hector through the window. Then he went outside and made Hector find my shoe and bring it back to me. He also forced Hector and his friends out of the park. The park was for little kids, according to my great-grandfather. The next time I saw Hector, he said, "Listen, there's no problems. I was just joking. Tell Mr. Dean we're cool." I remember seeing this all happen and thinking, "Whoa, that's respect."

So both my great-grandparents had a big impact on my childhood. They taught me discipline, manners, self-respect. My father would come in and out. He was a musician, one of the DJs who started on Sedgwick Avenue (the birthplace of hip-hop) along with DJ Kool Herc. I got my love for music and the passion to perform from him. He was also very humble, very laid-back. I have a similar calmness.

I was thirteen when Bubba passed away, and I was getting a little wild. By that time, my mother had married a man named Andre King, and so I was with them on the other side of the Bronx. He was a great stepdad to my brother, Damien, and me. I saw him and my mom work extra hours just so we (soon to include my baby brother, Andre Jr.) would have everything we needed. He and Mom always made sure we had good Christmases and birthday parties. We had our school uniforms, clothes, and family trips. They provided for every celebration. My stepfather also provided the ass whoopings when needed. A few were definitely needed. I was getting into too much trouble in the Bronx, getting into fights in the neighborhood and at school. It got to the point where my stepdad and my father sat down together and came up with a solution: my stepfather, who worked for the post office, got a transfer to Atlanta, and we all moved there. I don't doubt that if not for that move, I'd be in jail or dead.

These three men, along with my mother, of course—they protected me, they provided for me, and they put me in the position I'm in now. Everything I saw my great-grandfather, father, stepfather, and uncles do, it's now on me to do. I have that responsibility—to take the respect, strength, and unity they showed me and build on it for the next generation. And that's what I'm on to now.

PURPOSE-DRIVEN

I've got five kids, and I love them. It doesn't matter when or how they entered my life. They all changed my life. They gave me more drive. Way more drive.

When I was a kid, Mable would take me to the grocery store and tell me to go help people pack their bags at the register. There I was, helping Miss Barbara or Mr. So-and-So—folks my great-grandparents knew. And then someone would give me a quarter. Someone else would give me a dollar. It was just coins on the counter. When I added up the tips from that first day, I showed the twenty-something dollars to my great-grandmother, and she said, "You do good things for people, good comes back to you. You should continue doing that." So on weekends, I'd get up early and work several regis-ters at the C-Town from about eight in the morning to three o'clock in the afternoon. I'd make as much as five hundred dollars a day, but I didn't do it for the money. I was just raised to help people out. I'd turn the cash over to Mable, and if there was something in particular that I wanted, it came out of that stash.

Music was kind of the same thing. I started dee-jaying parties when we moved to Atlanta because I loved being in front of a crowd. Whatever money I made was spent getting more records so I could be in front of a crowd even more. I never really had a cash-out plan with music, like, "Okay, how am I going to get rich off of doing this?" My focus was always "How am I going to continue to have fun do-ing this?"

So when I say that my kids gave me more drive, I'm not talking about the drive to make money simply to have money. Sure, I'm going to set them up financially, but only so they have something to pull on, so that they can continue to grow. But money itself shouldn't change your mental attitude. The amount you have might affect what kind of dinner you eat for a particular period of time. But you can't let something that comes and goes change your understanding of life. I know what it feels like to not have money. I've been broke and rich a hundred times. The world spins on real things. And you definitely have to pass down more than material things.

The drive I have now stems from the fact that my kids are watching me and will someday follow my example. Just how I soaked up street smarts from the men in my family and mixed in business experience and a Harvard education, my children are going to grow into what I give them and figure out how to take it to the next level to make it their own.

The drive I have now stems from the fact that my kids are watching me and will someday follow my example. Just how I soaked up street smarts from the men in my family and mixed in business experience and a Harvard education, my children are going to grow into what I give them and figure out how to take it to the next level to make it their own.

REAL TIME, REAL LOVE

Anybody can take their kid out and buy him or her a pair of sneakers. Anybody can mail a child support check. Not everybody will step up and be a father. Not everybody is going to protect, provide, and inspire. We're missing the fathers who are coaches—who are training the next generation. I want to be the father who builds and then teaches his kids how to continue building. Securing that solid foundation with your kids takes energy, consistency, and time.

And that's where the issue of blending is key. The type of father I need to be requires time with my children. And time is not something you can ever get back. You might be going through something with your child's mother, and that might look like an obstacle between you and your child. But never compromise your time with your kid over a disagreement or a dispute that has nothing to do with the kid. Too often, a guy might say to his child's mom, "You know what? Screw it. If you don't want me to see my son, he'll grow up and understand that absence was your fault." But there is absolutely no guarantee your kid is going to interpret the situation in that way. All you might be left with is your ego and lost time.

When I was younger, I had a vision of what my family would look like. The old people used to tell me all the time, "You got to get yourself some stability. A wife, some kids, a home." And I took that advice seriously. Growing up, I was hyperaware of my surroundings. I didn't let myself trust too many people. I saw too many things go down, so I was always on my toes. This was also true when it came to relationships. I might think, "Hmmmm, that girl is pretty," but I'd also notice how she set up two guys to get robbed. I didn't want to take that chance. But at the same time, I didn't want to be alone either. I would see guys become successful and go to drugs or just not make it all the way. I figured it out: if you have all this money, all this freedom, and no boundaries, you're going to crash. So I got a woman I could trust in Mashonda, and the next step was to make a home and have kids. With that in hand, I would graduate from boy to man.

Mashonda had a tough pregnancy with Kasseem. She was in the hospital on bed rest for two or three months. When I got the call that my son was going to be born that day, I was in such a good mood. I was so excited for Mashonda and so excited for myself that I got dressed up in a suit to go to the hospital. When the doctor saw me, she just shook her head and handed me scrubs. But showing up in the suit was something Bubba, my great-grandfather, would have done. The prince was coming, and his welcome was to be respected.

I thought I was living my vision. But we can't really paint the future as much as we think we can.

Separation is hard. We're humans; we get attached to things and to people. Anytime you're a part of something for ten years, or even five years, becoming unattached is not an easy process. I never planned to be apart from Mashonda, so I didn't know how to even approach it. I always thought I could fix our problems. But we got to the point where it couldn't be fixed. I didn't have the rules on how to break up. So it was painful. For her and for me. I think most people think it's not also difficult for men going through a time like this, but it is.

Our transition was complicated by emotions—my emotions and her emotions. And in the middle of it was KJ. My relationship with Mashonda was over, but the son we had created together still remained.

One thing I give Mashonda credit for is that during the years when we were working out how best to co-parent, she never held Kasseem from me. We never argued around him; we never yelled around him. KJ never had to cry out, "Mommy, stop," or "Daddy, stop." Still, kids are going to pick up on energy. All this fake dropping-off here and the "All right, see you later" stuff? Kids know what's real and what's fake. KJ sensed that Mashonda and I weren't being real with each other. He started asking questions. He'd ask me, "Why can't my mom come and see my room?" We didn't have good answers for questions like that.

But we all recognized that our conflicts—though never acted out in front of KJ—were affecting our son. He's an amazing kid who can perform at 100 percent, but because we weren't handling our business, he was stuck at 60 percent. And it wasn't his fault. We didn't want our lack of unity to spread like a virus among the brothers.

ELEVATE THE CONVERSATION

Mashonda, Alicia, and I all decided we needed to refocus on communication and unity. We started meeting at my studio office, hammering out solutions at the table, having real conversations. These were elevated conversations where all parties had to park their egos outside the door. You couldn't come into the room believing you were doing a favor for the other person. You're supposed to do what it takes to create the best environment for your child. No one could bring a sense of entitlement into the conversation either. Everybody had to show up as equals with good intentions.

In the early days, we brought in people who were familiar with the situation. We had mediators, which I recommend to anyone serious about resolving conflict. All of us alone couldn't have the right conversation. A mediator helps everybody get through the sticky parts. A mediator can be anyone, as long as they are fair (without preconceived notions) and open and ideally have love for everyone in the room. My uncle was a great asset in those early days because I respect him, Mashonda respects him, and he respects us both. He said very few words, never intruded on the process. But sometimes just listening can be mediation. With my uncle in the room I was able to say things I might not have, and he was able to keep us all focused. It takes a half second to tune out of a conversation.

My wife has also always been instrumental in helping me stay open, understanding, and positive. One of the tools she suggested that worked very well in our meetings was the "no interruption" rule: each person gets a chance to speak their truth exactly how they see it. You might disagree, but you don't interrupt. You let that person finish their thought, and after they are done, then you reply. It helped us to really listen and learn from one another. Before that, we all talked over one another and didn't leave learning anything. The "no interruption" rule set the precedent for respect.

Setting the tone and monitoring the vibe is key. One person with an attitude could spread their bad vibe to everybody, which leads to an unproductive meeting. As soon as negativity walks into the room or answers the phone, reset the zone. You could do this by rescheduling ("Listen, let's not even do this today") or talking it through. Talking it through requires that you keep the tone simple: "Hey, I didn't really mean that, and you aren't really saying this, right?" "No, I didn't mean to do that. And when I did this, I was really trying to do this, not that." You do this back-and-forth until everybody gets even, cools down. This method works in the streets and when dealing with spouses. If you know how to communicate and reset the zone, you could turn any misunderstanding into mediation.

Sometimes you're the one whose vibe is off. Right after the divorce, I was content knowing that I could provide for my kids and be a good dad. Sure, I didn't get along with Mashonda, but I wasn't focused on finding a solution to that. Any arguments, any drama, I'd put in a box and head into the studio, and it would be as though the dispute didn't exist. But as time continued and I matured as a person, I started to take stock of a lot of things. Returning to school definitely accelerated this. I had always been someone who woke up with positive intentions, sometimes even going out of my way to make someone happy. But I began to really examine the impact I had on other people.

I started to think, "If there's a water leak in a ceiling, the plaster is going to have to soften for the water to get through." I decided I needed to soften.

When you're at an impasse, why wait for the other person to get things straightened out before you get your own stuff straight? Be the start of the healing. If you set the tone for the things you want to go in a positive way, you will create a domino effect, and everybody will come over to your way of thinking.

Blending means that all parties are amicable, understanding, and respectful. Liking one another is the final step. We started to identify the negative feelings and misunderstandings so that we could begin to let them go. We might have moments when we disagree, moments when Mashonda may not like me very much, moments when I might not like her that much. But we expect to like each other again the next day; we trust that vibes and attitudes will shift in a positive direction. Blending will be a family project forever because everyone involved is an individual with personalities, goals, and energies that constantly shift. But they shift within a unified structure.

There is power in the unity that comes from blending. The kids are always watching. When the adults are all on the same page, a kid might get a phone call from his mom, dad, and stepmom about the same thing. He knows for sure the blended thing is happening. Mashonda and Alicia, being on the same page, seeing eye to eye, being partners on a cause that is bigger than all of us, are the ultimate Krazy Glue that keeps our blending together. I had nothing to do with that. I couldn't negotiate their bond. Both of them wanted to speak for herself. Women are the world's healers. They have that gentle touch, that gentle sensitivity, to handle it. A guy has no business in the middle of it.

GROWN-UP MOMENTS

Blending doesn't happen overnight. It's difficult work, and there are times when the dynamic will shift, the consistency will dip. In the meantime, behave as though everything between you and your co-parent is good. You may not like your ex at a particular time, but let your kid see you behaving with love toward that person. If it's her birthday, take your kid to get his mother a gift. Not just any gift—add extra stuff. It's not being fake; take it as exercising while your feelings can catch up.

Sometimes you'll get stuck on a particular thing. Especially men. You think to yourself, "I don't want to do this/pay for this/go to this place." But you have to take your ego off the table sometimes and bite the bullet. Will you be able to see your kid at the end of the day? If so, you still win.

It's tricky to take your ego off the table without feeling disrespected, but you can craft it so you feel comfortable. Weigh your sacrifice against the mental or physical damages to your child or your relationship with your child. For example, what if my daughter's mother enrolled her in basketball camp? Maybe I preferred she play soccer. Her mother knows I love soccer, played soccer all my life, and the soccer field is closer to my office so I could see her play. Enrolling her in basketball camp is a power move on her mother's part, and I could easily be disgusted and refuse to go to any games. But what is the effect on my daughter if I skip all the games?

This is what I call "taking a grown-up moment": look at the long view and take the perceived loss, because it's the most adult-like thing to do. As men, we have to take more grown-up moments if we want them in return. Once you have about five grown-up moments under your belt, you can bring that up: "Listen, you know I didn't really want to do this, but I did. And I did this. I did that, and I did that. It's probably your turn to be a grown-up as well, right?"

Women, being more mature than men, naturally have more grown-up moments. But what messes them up is that they are more emotional. Instead of focusing on the grown-up moment at hand, they bring up something from ten years ago that throws off the tone and kills the grown-up moment. We've found that if we keep it on the grown-up moment itself, we'll get forward movement on things.

Oftentimes people use money to get stuck in a corner. A guy will complain that he's being pressed beyond what he can do financially. A woman might decide to not let the children see their father if he's not regular with support payments. Both parties are focused on the wrong thing. I know a lot of billionaires who are making a mess of parenthood. I know people who don't have any money but who go above and beyond to make sure their kid has everything.

The best money I've ever spent was on my kids. Not on the latest gadget but on experiences that will help shape their future. Your kid can have an experience sitting next to you on a park bench, and that doesn't have to cost a thing.

Withholding a child because of money is just a tactic. Using money to maintain a dispute is shortsighted. Letting finances stop the flow between you and a child is the worst mistake. These are problems with the inner person; these are problems with a person's intentions. When we leave this world, we can't take one material thing. The only thing we leave behind is our impact.

MY LIFE'S LOVES

My firstborn son, Nasir, is now a teenager, living in Miami. He acts like me, talks like me, moves like me, even tries to pull the same things I did. When I look at him, I'm still blown away that he even exists. He's the third-generation DJ in our family and could have added "Beatz" to his moniker, but he's playing a different type of music, wanting to graduate from what I did to something all his own.

Kasseem lives with us for one day out the week and every other weekend, and with his mom, Mashonda, the rest of the time. He's the stellar guy we always knew he would be, once his mother and I straightened out our agenda.

My daughter, Nicole, is so sweet and so smart. She lives in London with her mom, loves cars, and wants to be the first black female Formula One driver. She's my twin, and I'm trying to figure out how I'm going to behave having a daughter and letting her have her space to grow up.

And, of course, there are my babies with my wife, Egypt and Genesis. Egypt is a magnet for creativity, naturally gifted. In fact, he produced his first track for the rapper Kendrick Lamar when he was five years old—one of my best dad moments ever. Genesis is the little boss. He's going to run the whole family in a minute.

I'd love for all my kids to live with me all the time. That would be my bliss: just to wake up every morning and gaze on these gifts from God. I want the five of them to love and learn from one another. That would not be possible if we didn't make blending a family goal. We have such a short time on Earth, and I want to consume every moment with my loved ones. Because you're never going to get back a second, or a minute, an hour, a day, a week, or a month.

CHAPTER 6

Walk in Empathy

I n many discussions about raising a child after a divorce, the question often asked is "When should I introduce my child to someone new?" I think that answer is one that is truly personal to the parents involved. There is no hard-and-fast rule. The key factor is your state of mind. What's the temperature of your emotions? What is your capacity to be empathetic?

THE EGO IS A LIAR

The point at which one partner has moved on to love another is often the moment when tempers flare and negativity dominates the conversations between separated parents. We might tell ourselves that the new partner is a "danger" to our child, that he or she would neglect or resent our child. We might worry that our ex, wrapped up in a new love, might leave our child behind. Or we may fear losing our child to this new person.

These concerns spring from the ego, not the spirit. Let me tackle the faulty thinking behind these fears one by one. Your child's parent wants what is best for the child. Why would he or she invite someone in the child's life to do them harm, someone who wasn't an appropriate caretaker? I know that this may seem difficult to deal with because this person is a complete stranger to you. However, we have to give the benefit of the doubt in these moments; we have to think, "What if the shoe was on the other foot?" The day will come when you are ready to bring a new person into the equation and will want your ex to be accepting of it.

In introducing the child to the significant other, the parent is seeking to integrate the child into the new partner's life. This is active involvement, not disengagement. The parent is asserting that he or she wants to continue to be an active parent. This should be embraced, not challenged or refused. I'm sure we've all heard about a parent finding a new love and disappearing from their child's life altogether. A true nightmare for any young soul to live through. In instances like that, it's a good idea to seek a therapist for your child.

As to the fear of losing your child, I'll discuss this particular anxiety in more detail in the next chapter. For now, please recognize that your child is not your property. He or she is not a trophy to be won or lost. Children may be smaller than us in size, but their human experience is just as significant. We must allow them to experience most things freely and without judgment or criticism.

I don't want you to think that I'm dismissing feelings of distrust or anxiety. They "feel" very real in that moment, but it's the ego that is keeping you stuck in that place. Most of the time, we create drama around the presence of a new partner because we are simply unable to face the truth that our ex has moved on to someone new. The way out of these insecurities, this fear, is by accepting "what is" and recognizing the power of "letting go." Instead of worrying about what's not yours anymore—that dream of the perfect, traditional family—be grateful that you have this beautiful, healthy child you get to raise as a full, loving human being. In these moments, think of all that you do have and envision your future the exact way that you want it.

A KIND INTRODUCTION

From early in our separation, Swizz and I made a pact to introduce a new significant partner to each other. As his relationship with Alicia progressed, I knew the day she would meet my son, Kasseem, would come. I prayed about this day beforehand. How would it feel to sit across from my ex-husband and Alicia with our small child by my side? I worried about Kasseem being confused or sad. Would he get angry or pick up on the energy? I told myself this was happening for a higher good. I knew that if I felt awful about it, Kasseem would sense my energy and feel awful too. Children are so pure, they respond to good intentions and can feel negativity from a mile away.

We agreed to meet at a restaurant and have dinner. I asked Kasseem's godfather, Chad Elliott, to accompany me. Chad is a close friend to both Swizz and myself, so I knew he would bring balance to a room full of awkwardness. It's good to have a neutral person at your side during occasions like this, someone both parties trust. Having this person as a safety net will help you navigate through the emotional challenge of being there.

When we walked in, Swizz and Alicia were already sitting down. Kasseem ran over to his dad and hugged him. We had agreed that I should tell Kasseem beforehand that Alicia was Daddy's girlfriend. I believed that hearing it come from me would make him less resistant to the idea of his dad having a new companion.

I told Kasseem he should go sit with his dad and Alicia, and he looked back at me to make sure it was okay. Swizz placed him in the middle seat, and Alicia looked at him with amazement. A fixed stare full of admiration and enchantment. She told him how handsome he was. It was very endearing, very believable. Her energy toward him was good.

From my intense observation over the course of dinner, it seemed Alicia genuinely liked Kasseem. Watching Kasseem sit with Swizz and Alicia so comfortably, I felt an emptiness come over me. My son was experiencing something I had wanted to give him as a woman and a mother. I was fully aware that this could very well be the rest of my life, playing out there, at that table. Me, my son, and what I had to accept as his "new family."

The introductory meeting was a success, so much so that Swizz asked me if Kasseem could go home with them that night. At first I choked on the air in my lungs and my heart fell an inch deeper into my chest. Then, I took a deep breath and remembered why I was there. I wanted to be fair to Swizz. I knew this was healthy for Kasseem.

And having seen for myself how in tune Alicia was with my son, I knew he was safe.

IN HER SHOES

Empathy is the decision to step into another person's perspective. It is the antidote to ego because it replaces the "me" and the "I" with "you."

When Alicia met Kasseem and me for that dinner, empathy played a tremendous role. I was able to put myself in Alicia's shoes because I remembered how vulnerable I felt meeting Swizz's oldest son for the first time. When he was born, Mum told me with memorable conviction, "If you love Swizz, you must love his child as if he's your own." I understood what this meant right away, so I took heed to the advice my grandmother provided. I knew that he wasn't my child, but in his little face, I saw Angel, the son I lost, and I saw my future children with Swizz. This child was a gift and as adults we must remember that children don't ask to be here. They enter our lives with great purpose and they deserve to be treated with selfless, egoless love.

Because of my experience with Swizz's oldest son, I knew that it was possible that Alicia would put her best foot forward in taking care of Kasseem. I recognized this similarity: we were both women willing to love and care for a child who didn't come from our own wombs.

Recognizing a similarity in another person is the first step toward empathy. If you can identify how you and another are alike in character or circumstance, then you can begin to imagine the situation from his or her perspective. Empathy is not simply about caring for another person. It is placing yourself in a mental and emotional position to feel what they are feeling. Empathy is using your imagination to adopt another person's perspective and becoming sensitive to the experiences that have influenced that perspective. If you are fully immersed in the act of empathy, there is literally no room for your own emotions, feelings, and prejudices.

The ego won't like this and will try to undermine your efforts by whispering in your ear, "You have nothing in common with this person," "You can't possibly understand her," and sometimes even "You are much better/much worse than him." Don't listen to the ego. The truth is that human beings are divinely designed to connect with one another. Once we set aside judgment, we can find the link with the other person and build a foundation.

Empathy requires work, and it may seem like a lot of effort to some women and men; these are often the same people who claim they don't need to have a relationship with their ex's new partner. I recognized that Kasseem's life was about to change, and so it was imperative that I understood the new woman in my son's life.

During our discussion about this book, Dr. Shefali explained that how a child perceives a new romantic relationship depends on how the parents contextualize things for the child: "It can be a very beneficial thing for the child to have different and new people in their lives. If the introduction is done in the spirit of empowerment and transformation, everyone can benefit from it. If both parents are inclusive, nonjudgmental, and nondivisive, the children will follow suit." How you prepare yourself and your child for an introduction to a new person matters.

Rather than taint their pure energy with our own baggage (distrust, resentment, fear), we should work toward embracing their innocence. Let the children lead us toward love.

Sheree shared the beautiful story about the first time her son, Trey, met his father's then girlfriend, Jada. Will called beforehand and told Sheree that he was going to introduce Trey to Jada that weekend. Sheree appreciated the heads-up. After four-year-old Trey returned home, she asked him about the visit, but "not an interrogation. Just a general question about whether he had fun at his dad's house." Trey told her that he met "Miss Jada" and that she "was so nice to me." He asked if they could buy her a present. Sheree recognized her son's pure heart. Not only did they give her a present, Sheree added a card, in which she thanked Jada for making such a good impression on her son.

This is a prime example of letting empathy lead you to kindness and gratitude from the very start. In this case, Sheree took on her son's perspective. By giving the gift, Sheree not only empowered the child to receive and give love to Jada, she also set a tone for her relationship with Jada. "The card was an olive branch. The land was tilled; the foundation was prepared and set."

If parents do not take deliberate steps to prepare themselves or their child for an introduction, the results will likely be less successful. Avoidance is never the route to take. Take as an example Taharqa Patterson, a musician who now lives in northern New Jersey. He was two years old when his parents divorced and easily moved between both parents' homes. When Taharqa was seven, his mother moved from Harlem to Chicago. He returned to New York to spend happy holidays and entire summers with his father. When he was around eight years old, he called his dad's house and a woman answered the phone. He didn't think it was appropriate to ask who she was (since he was a young child), and she didn't think to introduce herself. Taharqa had, in fact, never been aware of his father dating anyone. His father had never exposed that aspect of his life to his son. When Taharqa landed at the airport for that summer, Christine was sitting in the car.

There was never much of a conversation about Christine between father and son, except that his father told him she was "someone special." The father and son pair, who had spent summers attending concerts, hanging out at the recording studio, and throwing a Frisbee, now became a threesome. The fact that the dynamic shifted so suddenly burdened the relationship between stepmother and stepson. When his father left for a two-week tour, these two people who were essentially strangers to each other were left to wing it through the rest of the summer. It was awkward and sometimes tense, and their chemistry remained off for several years.

EMPATHY TOWARD THE CHILD

As important as it is for adults to be empathetic toward each other, it is key that the adults be empathetic toward the children. Children are not little people; they are future people being molded. They did not ask to be born. They did not ask for these massive shifts in their family structure. Dr. Shefali suggests that we as parents can minimize the emotional impact of a separation by reducing the amount of conflict and inconsistency that our child is exposed to. But we should also allow them to express their distress about the changes openly and honestly. These empathetic conversations will allow you to fully acknowledge the disruption to your child's life, while also making your child feel less isolated in the whirlwind that happens during a separation. Kasseem was very young when he met Alicia, but I was still sure to talk with him about the meeting before it happened. An open conversation beforehand and a follow-up check-in afterward help the child understand that this is a topic that they can freely discuss.

Empathy from you, the parent, ultimately becomes empowerment for the child. In order to compensate for the tremendous shifts that have occurred in a child's life without his or her consent, Dr. Shefali advises that parents introduce more autonomy into the child's life. In Dr. Shefali's opinion, a typical ten-year-old child is old enough to decide where he or she wants to live full-time and when to visit the other parent. "Perhaps set a mandate for a visit once a month, or allow the child to decide whether she wants to stay for one night or two nights. Graduate the amount of choice the child has, instead of sticking to a court mandate," she suggests. Michelle Seelinger, entrepreneur and philanthropist, no longer has a specific visitation schedule in place for her daughters. She and her ex-husband, David, found that forcing visits created problems for the girls and between the two of them: "Instead, my ex and I always make sure the girls know they are wanted by both of us at any time. We don't make either child feel badly for wanting or *not* wanting to spend time with either of us. The girls are able to make up their own mind when it comes to when and if they want to be with me or their dad."

This flexibility requires that both parents have cooled egos. Rather than feel hurt that a child may decide not to spend as much time with a parent, that parent can use this information to think about what he or she is doing that is not attracting the child to visit.

Remember also that blending is a continuous process. Empathy does not end after the first or second introduction. Children constantly evolve, and as they mature and gain deeper insights about themselves and their surroundings, continue to check in with them. Dr. Erica Reischer, author of *What Great Parents Do*, reminds parents that sometimes kids aren't able to express their feelings or don't know that things are out of whack. Use your parental intuition, and observe your child. Are they still enjoying things they have enjoyed before? Are they complaining about physical pains or aches?

Spending time being with your child, being open and sensitive to what they are feeling, is essential. Often parents notice their child is having difficulties and want to jump in to fix things. "Don't fix their feelings," Dr. Reischer explains. "It's more productive to simply acknowledge your child's feelings; the acknowledgment will make him or her feel validated and important. It is also important for children to learn how to tolerate hard feelings. Your child is more likely to realize that feelings eventually shift and develop positive coping strategies if you don't rush to execute a rescue."

When Malik Yoba's three children were younger, he spent time with his friends when he had his kids. "I was of the mind-set, 'If I'm going to have my kids around people, they're going to be good people. My kids are gonna grow from being around them.'" His ex wasn't happy about this. She wanted Malik's time with his children to just be him and the kids. He saw this as her trying to tell him how to parent, and so he resisted. Now he knows that he didn't always get it right. "I thought I was doing the right thing, and now they tell me, 'No, Dad. We just wanted you. We didn't want to be around your friends.' I had to learn that what I thought was reasonable was often quite unreasonable in their minds. I should have listened more often."

Embracing your child's perspective does not mean that you submit to all your child's whims and wants. You are still the parent, entitled to live your truth and obligated to guide your children. Sheree described this delicate balance, saying, "You never want to undermine your child's feelings. Their feelings are very real, so you will want to validate them. But sometimes there is a side of a situation they are not seeing. Sometimes we only can track what we're losing or what is missing from our lives. But this is a lack mentality. Always encourage your child to see what they are gaining because of the situation."

> **"How does blending change as the child gets older? Is blending even necessary if my child is fifteen when we divorce?"**
>
> Even after our children grow into adults, they need functioning parents to support and love them. They need us to be present and in a peaceful state during all their milestones—graduations, weddings, holidays, etc. We should want to be happy and on one accord in order to help them raise their children. There is no age limit to blending. If your child is requesting it, that is reason enough for you to attempt it.

CLEARING THE PATH FOR NEW BONDS

Studies say that it takes about four years for a blended family to gel properly. Often the early interactions between the adults and the children can determine whether the road ahead is bumpy or smooth. If the adults can commit to showing empathy to one another, it's much more likely that everyone will have a more pleasant experience. Children in successfully blended families are the ultimate winners: they learn flexibility and enlarge their social as well as their family circles.

I had accepted that Swizz was no longer my husband, and I had moved on. Once Alicia came into Kasseem's life, I had to jump over a different hurdle. I had to accept that my son could be loved by another parental figure.

After Swizz and Alicia married, Kasseem began referring to Alicia as Umi, which means "mother" in Arabic. They didn't like the way "stepmommy" felt, and from personal experience, I agreed. Stepmothers since the time of Cinderella have gotten a bad rap. And on the flip side, Granny Sandra would say that a stepmother was someone who "stepped" in to raise a child for a parent who wasn't there. But no one was stepping into my place.

I hear women say things like "I don't want my child to forget me" or "I don't want my baby to like this other woman more than me." Even if it's not said out loud, it's still a thought that subconsciously runs through a mother's mind.

I understand the phobia that lives in these feelings. As a mother, you want your children to look at you as though you're their everything, their only queen, their goddess. While this sounds great, it's just not realistic. Love is love. Our children will grow up and experience relationships with hundreds of different people. And we must allow them that freedom to openly love others. We must empower this strength.

Allowing your children to be loved by other adults benefits them in ways you might not expect. When Taharqa was fifteen, his mother began dating the man who would become his stepfather. "I had been playing football for the better portion of my life. And he was coaching football. My father was not an athlete. He is a musician, a music nerd. But my stepfather could engage with me on that athletic level. Football was such a central part of my everything at that time. Honestly, I started playing as a way to blow off steam, and my stepfather understood that. He and my mom drove for four hours every weekend I had a game. In many ways, he rounded off my life. We were tight right from the beginning, and we still are today."

So I stepped back and took a deeper breath. I sat down and spoke to Kasseem about calling Alicia Umi. I'll never forget how he looked at me and, with his tiny little voice, said, "I know you're my real mommy." Since Kasseem drew his first breath, I've dedicated my life to being present and of service to him. Even at four years old, Kasseem recognized this and honored it. I didn't need to feel threatened by Alicia showing him affection.

We have to stay mindful of the fact that we are raising individual souls. Yes, they are from our bodies, but they do not belong to us. We can't hinder their growth because of our own fears and insecurities. If you're doing your very best as a mother, that work will always speak for itself. Granny Sandra, who raised six of her own children, would tell me, "You got to keep Kasseem where he's so filled with love that he will excel at anything because he's happy. Be there for him. The more you're with him, the more time you spend with him, just you and him, the tighter the bond grows, so tight nothing can come between that."

Many parents avoid being around their child's bonus parent. Perhaps they can't confront what lingering awkwardness or fear remains. However, I've learned that seeing is believing, and believing leads to acceptance. What I've grown to recognize is that Alicia is a committed caretaker for Kasseem. Not only does she carefully maintain his schedule when he's in her home, she seeks to establish and fortify a bond with him by spending time with him individually, by showing up emotionally and physically for him. I remember when

Kasseem was in third grade, there was a parent meeting at his school. Swizz was unable to attend, and Alicia asked if she could accompany me instead. It wasn't something she had to do, but it showed me that she loved my son and was committed to him. Seeing is believing, and believing leads to acceptance.

Love is love. Our children will grow up and experience relationships with hundreds of different people. And we must allow them that freedom to openly love others. We must empower this strength. What I've grown to recognize is that Alicia is a committed caretaker for Kasseem. She has chosen to love him, and I'm grateful for this.

Kasseem knows without a doubt that I love him. But he expects me to love him because I'm his mother. Alicia is a woman who has chosen to love him, and I'm grateful for this. Along with empathy, gratitude is the most important piece of successful blending. Recognizing the way your children's lives are made better by the care and concern of your co-parent is a straight path to muzzling the ego and embracing happiness.

So is it possible to simply accept the care you receive from your co-parent's new significant other without developing a relationship with that person? I suppose it is. For me, it felt unnatural that my son looked at another woman as a mother figure when I wasn't present and I had absolutely no relationship with her. It was time to bridge the gap.

CHAPTER 7
Bridging the Gap

Kasseem wanted Alicia and me to like each other. When he was at his dad's house and we were on the phone together, he would wait until I was finished talking and then say, "Mommy, do you want to say hi to Umi?" He's such a slickster, that kid. He always knew just what he needed and wanted for his life and was determined to manifest it. Sometimes we would just get on the phone and exchange a few words because we knew Kasseem was listening and analyzing every second of our interaction.

DEAR UMI, WHO ARE YOU? WHO ARE WE?

In the early days of co-parenting, Alicia and I were not yet friends; we did not meet by choice. In situations where you are put in such close proximity with another human being, you really have to sit back and ask yourself, "What am I supposed to learn from this person I so strongly feel detached from?" It is often the case that the people and situations you don't expect to enter your life are the ones that teach you the greatest lessons. I didn't completely understand at that time how a relationship with Alicia would play itself out, but through my self-work, I'd learned and understood the importance and value of accepting what life put in my path rather than resisting it.

By the end of 2012, I was ready to build a new relationship with her. During a phone call to discuss some of the details of Kasseem's upcoming sixth birthday party, I asked Swizz to extend my personal invitation to Alicia, and he did. And she accepted.

Alicia stayed until the very end. It was our first time being in a setting together for so long, smiling joyfully and enjoying ourselves. The day after the party, she called to thank me for inviting her. There was a dramatic shift in our energy; it was new and hopeful. And then she said, "Let's connect. Let's have dinner." I agreed, but I felt incredulous that we were at this point. The afternoon before our dinner, I felt that I was going to meet Alicia, the woman, for the first time. Not Alicia Keys, the artist in the music videos banging out records that have made her a music icon to our generation. There was so much on my mind, so much I needed to tell her if our relationship was to become authentic and solid. The gate was open, and we were going to use this as an opportunity to search each other's soul. But it was so new, so fragile.

During this period, my ask of God was simple: "Please provide the tools that I need to move through whatever presents itself." I felt that asking for something specific wasn't my place. Many times in life, we don't know exactly what we need. But I believe my Creator always does know. I imagined receiving a little toolbox filled with everything I needed to get through the challenges—which words to speak, when to speak them, and when to simply listen. I put my faith in the divine toolbox.

EMPOW*HER*

I hear women say all the time:

> "I don't need to be friends with his girlfriend/wife."

> "We don't need to like each other."

> "She just better do right by my child."

Those are all major misconceptions. If your child is telling you that his or her father's new significant other does right by him or her, honor that. Show gratitude. She doesn't have to do anything for your child. And for your child's sake and your own peace of mind, you should at the very least want to form a solid foundation that can become a safe place for communication and healthy interaction.

Too often, women are pushed into competition with one another—in school, in the workplace, and in our personal lives. This contentious spirit is at the core of many issues between a biological mom and a significant other. When the wall between the biological mom and the stepmom seems impossible to break through, it is often the case that the biological mother hasn't let go of the covetousness and infatuation that comes with wanting a man/partner who is no longer hers. It will be impossible to blend your family if any of these feelings linger.

If these feelings are not released, the woman is still bound emotionally. What's worse is that she will embed this energy into her child. The child might have an unexplained chip on his or her shoulder, animosity toward a stepparent and/or parent, or a feeling of displacement within his or her own family—all because of feelings that are the mother's and have nothing to do with the child. Is this fair to the child? Is this fair to anyone involved? No.

"My ex's girlfriend hates my daughter, and I don't understand why. Should I confront her?"

Misa Hylton, the mother of Sean "Puff Daddy" Combs's oldest son, Justin, had an excellent perspective on this situation. She said, "I'm a firm believer that you get back what you put out. The universe never lies. So if you're experiencing an energy that you don't like as it pertains to your child, you need to figure out why you're attracting it." Your negative feelings, no matter how hard you try to mask them, will land on your child, either because she will walk into her father's home with them or because his girlfriend is picking up on them. So search yourself first. Do you hate this woman? Even the word you used—"confront"—tells me that you're more prepared to battle than to understand. If you lead in creating a positive energy between the two of you, it's likely your child will be treated that way as well.

BUILDING A BRIDGE

People often say "Don't burn bridges" and "It takes a village to raise a child." These popular aphorisms are not used at the same time. But the moment I decided to consciously blend, both sayings brought a lot into perspective. The "gaps" between women and mothers, men and fathers, mothers and fathers are created when bridges are burned, when miscommunication or misunderstanding creates a heightened experience of distrust or resentment. In order for my blended family to work, I not only had to bridge the gap that was present between Alicia and me but I also had to welcome her into the "village" and allow the love and experiences that she was offering Kasseem to flow freely.

However, a bridge isn't built overnight. Again, the work starts with you because a bridge must have a strong foundation. Have you released all resentment? Have you fully accepted the path your life has taken? Have you learned to set ego aside in order to communicate openly and effectively? It was vital that I learned to stay present and not let the past or preconceived notions cloud my perceptions. Truth is, in the heat of the moments that disrupt our world, we tend to only remember the pieces of the story that serve our ego best instead of seeing the entire situation. But with forced awareness and continuous self-work, I was able to look at things with an eagle eye, very broadly and from up high. I practiced this method with every thought that I had about my team of family blenders, and I identified with them as only that—my new family. This enabled us to focus on mending and blending and avoid getting weighed down in negativity.

We had to show each other that we were sincere about taking only positive steps forward. Consistency was key. There were several small acts of kindness between us. Shortly after her first son was born, I gave her a copy of a book that I had cherished when I was pregnant, *100 Promises to My Baby* by Mallika Chopra. She started to send me flowers on my birthday, for Mother's Day, or after we had open communication meetings, always with touching messages included on the card. We were building our bridge.

GOLDEN GIRLS

The idea that a biological mother and a bonus mother can form a vital bond is pretty foreign in our culture. I visited many bookstores and websites in search of references that guided women on developing co-parenting skills regardless of the circumstances that surrounded their current or past relationship with the father of their children. The search was fruitless, possibly because there is inevitable awkwardness in the situation. We pressed through the awkwardness, and once it dissolved, we were able to set a positive tone in both households as a team, exponentially improving the probability for family success and mental wellness for generations to come.

The only other woman I knew at the time who had accomplished what I wished for with Alicia was my grandmother.

Smedley DuBoulay was my father's father. Mum said he was the most handsome man she ever laid eyes on and that he promised her love. Sadly, Smedley proved himself a storyteller. Once she got pregnant, he disappeared, and she didn't see him for several years. "He never gave me a dollar for bread to feed his son," she would say. She carried that hurtful memory with her for many years. They never had a relationship of any sort, and I sensed how it affected her.

However, Mum did form a relationship with Anita, the woman Smedley later married. I witnessed the bond between these women my entire life. Both women made sure their children knew one another and got along. There was no separation, no disconnect. They made us all practice love and unity. We were one. In the late nineties, they traveled the world together and shared in the joys of becoming grandparents and great-grandparents. The "Golden Girls," I called them. They became best friends, life partners. My grandmother sat by Auntie Anita's side the morning she died, and she cried to me that she had lost her friend and her sister.

Mum formed a solid friendship with the woman who would later marry my grandfather. She was my auntie Anita, and the two women focused on making sure their children knew one another and got along. There was no separation, no disconnect. They made us all practice love and unity.

During the nineties, Mum and Auntie Anita traveled the world together and shared in the joys of becoming grandparents and great-grandparents. They became best friends, life partners. Their relationship taught me so much.

Two women who had all the odds against them forming a friendship proved that they could still love each other regardless of any man, pride, or ego. I called them the "Golden Girls."

Their relationship taught me so much. Two women who had all the odds against them forming a friendship proved that they could still love each other regardless of any man, pride, or ego. They showed me that all they needed was to teach their children to love and grow with one another.

Underneath all the madness that the breakup, separation, and divorce brought into my life, there was a little girl who remembered the love that Mum and Auntie Anita shared, who witnessed their powerful dynamic firsthand. During the early part of this journey to blend my family, I realized that I was also blending myself. The experiences from my past were all surfacing. It was like the higher powers were opening me up to myself. The past had showed its purpose to my present, and the future became a vision of wholeness.

In the future, Alicia and I will become Golden Girls too.

I understood the power that all three of these time frames held, and it became my mission as a breathing soul to use everything I'd ever learned about life to evolve.

I was no longer that young girl; I stood in my own right as a grown, experienced woman. And I would walk in my grandmother's footsteps and create a loving relationship with Alicia. She was a woman just like me, a soul in human form, like I am. We deserved to be uplifted, to elevate one another. And because of the magic that I witnessed from Mum and Auntie Anita, I knew our children would prosper from it.

THE DIVINE FEMININE

Some people may wonder why I've applied so much focus on building a bridge with Alicia. This is an important question that gets to the core of how I understand, respect, and apply divine femininity.

I was raised by two women and have been loved, guided, and protected by positive female influences my entire life. I've always been hyperaware of the feminine energy that surrounded me. I enjoy it and respect it. What I know for sure is that women have superpowers and can fine-tune the vibrations of the world when we work together. Women are nurturers and collaborators, full of creative energy. We have a sacred connection to Mother Earth, and we have been gifted with the ability to manifest ideas, dreams, life, and existence itself.

Our culture lacks respect toward women and mistakenly looks

at femininity as a weakness or sexual distraction. As a result, many women have grown up to be very hard, disguising ourselves with a masculine shell in an attempt to protect our own bodies, our spirits, and our rights as humans. We've forgotten how to embrace our soft side because we always have our guard up.

While I was tending to my wounds shortly after the divorce, I specifically needed to awaken and align with my divine feminine core. I cultivated openness and love with everyone I came in contact with. I used guided meditations to cleanse negative energy. I burned sage and used rose, sandalwood, geranium, lavender, and peppermint oils medicinally. I also started collecting crystals and using them to set and hold positive intentions during meditations. I embraced my body and my sensuality, looking at myself as a piece of art, a sculpture—beautiful and original. Doing all these things to embrace my femininity, I began to feel lighter, safer, and more connected to myself. I gave myself permission to flow through life. And I recognized that it was key for moving forward.

Auntie Anita and Mum were drawn together because of their strong feminine cores. And it was the same divine feminine energy that fastened Alicia and me together on this journey toward blending. We slowly became vulnerable with each other. The more time that Alicia and I spent together, the more we were able to find a comfortable middle place for our souls to rest. We started to talk about everything. Our childhood, our grandmothers, and our children. We watched our children interact with one another: play with one another, fuss with one another, and then return to smiling and/or holding one another's hands. And in doing so, we gained a full awareness

of what our purpose was: that we were co-creators of a future generation rapidly growing right before our eyes—our sons.

The more time Alicia and I spent together, the more we were able to find a
comfortable middle place for our souls to rest. We started to talk about
everything. We watched our children interact with one another. And in doing so, we gained a full awareness of what our purpose was: that we were
co-creators of a future generation rapidly growing right before our eyes—
our sons.

MOTHERS UNITE

When women are able to open their hearts to one another and unite on a common goal, nothing is more powerful. Sheree's son, Trey, is now an adult, but when he was a child, she knew she could count on Jada to help get things done. Her primary link was Trey's father, Will. However, if he wasn't on top of a particular thing, she could just say, "Don't let me get Jada on you!" and Will would bust out laughing and say, "No, I got it. I got it." Sheree easily identified Jada as her ally.

Before Wendy, a successful entrepreneur, even went on a first date with the man she would ultimately marry, she knew he had two sons, Joshua and Adam, whom he loved very much. "They were part of the package, and I had no concerns about it, really. I love kids, and I thought that becoming their stepmother would be an interesting way to fast-forward my life into a role I knew I would be really good at. Kids always liked me."

Early on there was mild awkwardness between Wendy and the boys' mother, Joyce. Wendy would sit alone in the car while her future husband went to the door to pick them up, and there was no real engagement between the women. However, Wendy came to realize that this detachment had far more to do with Joyce's relationship to her ex-husband rather than a personal dislike of her. For Joyce, Wendy was essentially a bystander who did a great job taking care of her kids. When they had occasions to be around each other—family celebrations and such—both women were pleasant, if not overly warm, toward each other. Slowly and surely, their interactions increased.

When Wendy divorced her husband, the bond between her and Joyce grew: "I felt a generosity of spirit from her. Perhaps it was all in my head. I don't know. But in those early days, I felt that she knew what I was going through." Sadly, it was the death of her ex-husband that really cemented the bond between the two women. "My older daughter was a freshman in college, and my younger daughter was a freshman in high school when their father passed away suddenly from a massive heart attack. One of the boys was in California, the other was married. I was the one who got the call. Joyce was my first phone call, and it seemed we spoke every ten minutes. She and her husband came down from Boston. There were more than one hundred people at the funeral, and we stood together. As co-parents, as the team of moms that we had become over those many years. We each recognized, without ever stating it, that we were both mothers whose children had lost their dad. With that, we stood together." Years later, they danced together at their son's wedding. Wendy describes her relationship with Joyce as phenomenal, "totally loving and supportive.... There is nothing negative between us, just fluidity. We're a unit. She is most definitely a part of my family."

STEPPING INTO THE GAP

Sometimes, however, the relationship between a biological mother and a bonus mom doesn't start out well, and the gap seems impossibly wide. How does one begin to move into a productive, open relationship? Who should be the first to make an effort?

I actually think that either woman can begin, and as I've said throughout the book, the journey begins with a look inward. Misa didn't mince words: "Oftentimes, the biological mom may have unresolved issues with how the relationship ended, and when that happens, she might fall into the trap of creating issues that don't really exist. You can't find the best way to communicate, to co-create, or to co-parent when you have a chip on your shoulder."

Sometimes the bonus mom, feeling the weight of judgment or resentment from the biological mom, may volley back with petty strikes of her own. When Colleen began dating Vern, she asked if Vern's ex-wife, Cathy, wanted to speak to her, especially since the children were coming to visit her home. The word came back that Cathy had no interest in speaking with Colleen. A year later, just before Colleen and Vern were to marry, his ex-wife called Colleen's work number in an effort "to get to know her." Colleen couldn't engage with her during a busy workday and didn't feel compelled to speak with her: "At that point, I had gotten to know the kids. We had our own rapport. I thought to myself, 'I don't need to speak to you now just because you're ready.'"

It's essential that you identify your triggers. Many biological moms feel as though they are not being acknowledged, that their ex and the new partner are forgetting them, treating them as if they're not important. The bonus mom may actually feel something very similar—that her role as the new significant other is being disregarded and that her feelings are being overlooked. Sometimes she feels as if her own partner is not coming to her defense hard enough. There is a natural triangle between the biological mom, the father, and the child, and it's easy for the new partner to feel left out. When there is a lack of acknowledgment, respect, and inclusion on either side, the gap widens, lines are drawn in the sand, emotional walls are thrown up. The effort to overcome these things happens when either party (or both) exercise two things continuously: empathy and gratitude.

Misa had this to say: "I've been a baby's mother, I've been a wife, and I've been a stepmother. I've been on every side that you could think of. I always made the other women in my children's life feel as if they mattered. I followed their lead, their directions, what they wanted to happen with their child."

Making an effort to see the other person's perspective is the best way to understand their actions, and acting in accordance with your newfound understanding of their perspective on your behavior can defuse strife quickly.

It is likely that a biological mother has a history of friendship or affection with her child's father and can use that as a foundation for a positive relationship. Most likely, this is not the case between the biological mother and the bonus mom. However, their relationship can be built on gratitude. Misa reminds us to honor your child's bonus mom, saying, "When you have a woman who treats your child with love, who bathes your child, who cares for your child, who puts time in with your child, you have to honor that, appreciate that, and be thankful. Say thank you, because women do not have to do it, and there are women who don't." Saying thank you, as simple as it may seem, will break down barriers every time.

And from that point, what is left is patience. After the triggers have been identified, after the self-work has been done, when the heart has been switched to empathy and gratitude, the bonus mom and the biological mom can simply wait for an opportunity when the energy on both sides is receptive to deeper communication. For Alicia and me, this was Kasseem's sixth birthday party. We felt in that moment that a weight had been lifted, and we were ready to walk through in faith.

CHAPTER 8

The Divine Blueprint

I n March 2014, I headed to St. Barths with a girlfriend for some much-needed rest and relaxation. It was Kasseem's spring break, and I had dropped him at his dad's house so they could enjoy their week together. It just so happened that Swizz and Alicia had planned their family vacation at the same time on the same island. I never like to interrupt Swizz's time with Kasseem. I think it's important that a parent's time with his or her child be respected. However, Kasseem had never visited the island, and I really wanted to witness my baby boy in all his joy.

I called Swizz to ask if we could meet up so that I could see Kasseem. He told me he would get back to me; they had made some plans and just wanted to make sure it would work for everyone. I didn't take this the wrong way. My ego was under control. Plus, I understood what it's like to have plans with your child that you don't want to compromise. He called later and invited me to join them at Nikki Beach the next day. When I arrived, everyone was extremely kind and generous toward me. Kasseem played with his little brother, while Alicia, Swizz, and I sat on beach chairs talking and sipping drinks. The next thing I knew, out the corner of my eye I saw him lean in to kiss her. Did it feel weird? No, it didn't. This wasn't the first time I saw them display affection.

When I woke up the next day, the photo with Swizz kissing Alicia while I sat beside them was all over the blogs. Some of the articles celebrated the fact that the three of us were getting along; many were shocked that we were "vacationing together." Others seemed stuck on the fact that Swizz would kiss Alicia in front of me. We weren't vacationing together, like the media said. But it was the first time our blended family was on display.

A WINDOW, NOT A WALL

At the point when the picture was taken, the three of us had been working toward blending for about two years. I bring up the episode on the beach in St. Barths because it is a great example of one of the most beautiful benefits of blending—transparency. Blending means that there is a window between the two homes rather than an opaque wall. Each parent can look into the experience their child is having with the other parent, as opposed to having no input, no access, and no relationship.

These days, when we hire babysitters to watch over our infants, we install nanny cams in pillows so that we can make sure our children are safe. Daycare centers have rooms with one-way windows, where parents can peek in without distracting their child with their presence. Even when our children go to school, teachers these days are likely to have an open-door policy and are eager for parents to visit the classroom. Everywhere our children go, we expect to be there as their parents. But when they spend time at their other parent's home, we're supposed to send our children into a mystery box? Why should this be the case? We reject this in our family. There are times when Kasseem is home with me, and Swizz will call me and ask if he can stop by to surprise him. If the timing is right, I will allow these spontaneous moments to take place. Kasseem is always overjoyed to get the extra visit. Sometimes Kasseem misses his younger brothers and may want an impromptu visit to spend time with them at his father's house. I have no problem accommodating that.

When Sheree's son, Trey, was younger, there was a schedule in place, but they didn't adhere to it at all. "A schedule is a good thing to have in case you need it, but Trey would visit with his father whenever he wanted to. It was never a situation where we fussed about it. Trey needed to see his dad, and a schedule wasn't going to get in the way of this need."

Before we applied ourselves to creating a loving, blended family, I remember the feeling of emptiness that came over me every time my son left for his dad's house. I just couldn't get used to the regimen and felt little ease about the situation. I've always wanted to be there for all the firsts—big and small—in my son's life. But when you're co-parenting, that's just not realistic. I struggled with feeling left out.

When your child spends quality time with his or her other parent, you shouldn't feel a weird void or absence of purpose. Rather, you should feel as though you are doing what your child needs to become a well-rounded, family-oriented human. After the parents have created a new family relationship, communication can be free-flowing. Author Emma Johnson describes that as a huge benefit of blending: "Having an active co-parent helps you enjoy your children more. To be able to text a picture if they're doing something cute or tell your kids' dad, 'Look, they are learning how to ride a bike today.' It's joyful, and that trickles down into your kids." My co-parents and I talk, text, email, and exchange pictures all the time. We are committed to sharing those moments we know the other will appreciate.

We can also be a support to one another when things go horribly wrong. On New Year's Eve 2016, Kasseem traveled to Thailand with his father on a family trip. On the second day, I got a text from Swizz that read "Kasseem had a little accident." My heart dropped, and I immediately called Swizz. Kasseem had slammed his finger in a sliding door, and the tip had been severed. He put Kasseem on the line, and my heart nearly broke as I heard my brave boy try to assure me that he was okay. I felt powerless and lost. I wanted to be there to console him so badly, but my blenders truly came through. Swizz stayed on the phone with me until they arrived at the hospital and sent me pictures and videos throughout their time there.

When Swizz went in the room with Kasseem to get the stitches, Alicia stayed on the phone with me to calm me down and share with me how brave Kasseem was after the accident happened. Had the three of us not worked on our relationship, this entire situation would have been different. Maybe I would have received a text or phone call from halfway around the world and been forced to sit in worry until

I got an update later. Instead, Alicia pulled on the empathy that she has as a mother to understand what I would need in that moment. Our friendship kept her on the phone with me. She wanted to give me comfort, while Swizz gave full attention to our son. The last photo was of a smiling Kasseem showing me his neatly bandaged finger after getting seven stitches.

This is the peace that blending will bring you. Although I am sometimes absent, I am still well-represented and involved. I know that Kasseem is receiving double love.

The work Swizz, Alicia, and I have put into communication has released me from the anxiety I used to feel when Kasseem left my home for a visit with his father.

Now I can use the time apart from my son for personal renewal—to rest, read, and generally press the reset button. Emma encourages women to look at the time their children spend with their other parents as a gift, advising, "Now you have the time to go into the world, achieve in your career, date, exercise. Your children get to see you as the gorgeous, thriving woman you can be, not this stressed-out, angry mom who lacks support." Misa echoed the same thought: "I enjoyed the me-time. Single moms, especially, need to take advantage of having time away from their child." For me, the time Kasseem spent with his father made me a more relaxed, more loving mother to him when he returned.

THE DIVINE INGREDIENTS

Swizz, Alicia, and I have grown together on this journey toward blending, and it has made us better people. It was something we had to do for us and for our children. We've kept our flow private up until now but collectively decided to share our experience with the world because we know that what we've accomplished is something magical and that our testimony will help millions of families worldwide.

For most of this book, I've described how we got to this place: my personal efforts to heal and temper my ego, resetting my relationship with my former spouse by having those challenging conversations, and bridging the gap with his wife by practicing consistent acts of kindness on both sides.

However, blending is a continuous process. We are in a healthy place because we continue to do the work, filtering all our interactions through a set of principles that are the blueprint of our blended life. These are love, understanding, patience, compassionate communication, and boundaries. One is not more important than the other, and all five feed into one another.

> **"How do you get the extended family on board with the blending plan? My mother is way too pissed at my ex-husband to be welcoming to him."**
>
> When we're going through certain things with our partners, we can't help but vent to the people who care about us. And because they care about us, they will stand in judgment of our former partners. But I had a vision of my life being peaceful and carefree. I did what I had to do with my co-parents for myself, my sanity, and my peace of mind, as well as for my son and his well-being. Don't worry about getting your extended family on board. This type of work is between you, your co-parents, and your child. It isn't for everyone to witness or judge. You don't need outside opinions. Just do the work! Eventually your family and friends will follow your example.

LOVE

People are always asking me, "Are you guys just doing this for the kids, or do you really like one another?" My confident response is, "We not only like one another, we love one another!" This love, our awkward romance, is one that took eight years to blossom. The foundation is our centering love for Kasseem, which spread to a love of one another as his nurturers.

Swizz is now and will always be like my brother. He is someone I've watched grow from a boy to a man. We understand each other—our quirks, our desires, all our characteristics—very well. We're able to talk openly and with respect for each other.

The effort Swizz and I put into our relationship provided a clear path for Alicia and me to travel on our own terms, not forced by his will or his ideas of what our relationship should be. Alicia and I are future Golden Girls. We have developed something very honest and transparent. There is an energy between us that is sure and calm. It's more complex than a friendship. We are two women who will be conjoined by our children until the day we leave God's green earth. The parenting contract has been expanded. I am now a mother figure to her children because of the way they love and perceive their brother Kasseem. And she is a mother figure to Kasseem. This is a very intriguing connection, and we operate to bring honor to it. Working together, never against each other, makes life easier for us both. I know that she sees me, and I see her.

The three of us have developed a tradition to maintain this love: we hold hands and pray before every meeting, and at the end we always look one another in the eyes and say, "I am proud of you; I am proud of us."

UNDERSTANDING

As a child I would often hear Mum say, "Dear God, please grant me patience, wisdom, and understanding." My young mind didn't quite understand how the three worked together, but since she always asked for them in this order, I believed that there was magic in the combination. After living out my own experiences, I realized my grandmother wanted to understand not only others but herself.

Understanding yourself means knowing what motivates you, what your true goals and sources of joy are. This automatically elevates your behavior because you become focused on the bigger picture, the long view. It gives you the eagle vision I've already discussed. Self-understanding also means you've identified your emotional triggers, so you are more aware of your own thought process and can choose how to react to things, people, and conversations. When you understand yourself, it makes it easier to understand others. Self-regulation allows empathy, compassion, and peace to truly listen to another's perspective.

PATIENCE

Patience is one of the most self-gratifying virtues. At first, that might be difficult to understand because our culture pushes instant gratification. However, the ability to create peace in the moment of the unknown will save you from expectations, assumptions, and pain. Patience is an ongoing interaction with your higher self. Whenever I feel agitated that something isn't happening quickly enough, I imagine the universe whispering, "Hey, now's a good time for you to inscape. Go inward. Be still. Let me do my job."

In the earliest stages of blending, it's important to consider that just because you may be ready to go into full blend mode doesn't mean that your co-parent will be. Allow them the time to get comfortable, showing them that you are sincere and will do anything to make your child happy. It's important to remain positive and openhearted during this time.

When blending a family, you must also accept the fact that you are one part of a steadily moving machine, and like any machine, if one part of the device isn't operating optimally, it will cause a dysfunction and slow down the entire process. My co-parents and I make many decisions together—travel, holidays, visitations, and weekly itineraries. So it is not uncommon that any one of the three parents might need to wait for another parent to confirm their thoughts on a subject or plan. We strive to be gentle with everyone's feelings and give them time to be okay with new ideas and decisions. I might feel confident about a particular plan and not agree on pursuing an alternative. But we've all committed to respect each person's perspective. Respect does not mean that we agree with that perspective; rather, a sense of respect will help accomplish a middle ground between all parents.

Recently, I spoke to my son about what he thought was the key factor in the success of our family. He said, "Patience. Patience with everybody."

COMPASSIONATE COMMUNICATION

A key element of blending is what I describe as compassionate communication, which pulls together love, understanding, and patience.

When we allow love to guide our speech, emails, and texts, we open minds rather than close them. When we take a minute to do a self-check before we communicate with another person, making sure we're being inspired by our higher self and not our ego, we avoid inflaming the person to whom we're speaking.

Sheree emphasizes the importance of respect in communication: "As women, we have to watch our tone. Don't tell a grown person what they 'should' or 'shouldn't' do. Just take that word out of the conversation. It's too inflammatory." Sheree encourages all parties to learn how to communicate in a way that paves the way for peace and reconciliation. "You can't lose respect."

Our family is one that uses email and text a good deal. But even with such informal communication, we remember to start with "Hello, how are you?" That's something so simple, but it really helps to set a positive tone. Always think before you speak or type. Lead with facts, not opinions. And reread your message to make sure it feels right and to consider how the other person might receive it. If you feel strongly about something, there's nothing wrong with letting that be known, but remember to act from a place of self-control and grace. Remember, this is not about you and your emotions. By this point you've learned your triggers, and your emotions are under control. Don't get discouraged or upset if you don't get a response right away. This is an example of when you will need to exercise patience and understanding.

Parenting expert and author Amy McCready suggests that parents read specific parenting books together. Parenting is hard enough. If you are literally on the same page of a book, you'll have a shared language to use when discussing your children. There is a full list of recommended books in the Resources section of this book.

BOUNDARIES

This is a book about blending, but no group of people can successfully blend if healthy boundaries are not set in place. The goal in blending is communication, transparency, and a flow of positivity between co-parents. It is not meant to paint both homes with sameness. In fact, that is impossible. The ways in which each home is unique is a benefit for the child because it broadens his or her perspective and strengthens flexibility.

Boundaries are most certainly about respect. I acknowledge and respect that Alicia is the woman of her household. She, with Swizz, sets the rules there. Kasseem may spend time there, but the habits, rules, and ideas that I have established in my home don't arrive in the suitcase with him. This is a source of tension between many stepfamilies, and we'll return to this in the next chapter. For now, I will say this: your co-parents aren't babysitters; it's disrespectful for you to toss them a to-do list.

Misa Hylton is a very successful blender. Yet she remembers, in those early days, frustrating everyone because she wanted so much control over what happened with Justin when he was in his father's home, which Puff shared with his then girlfriend, Kim Porter. "I wanted her to make sure that his homework was done. I wanted him to come back the way I sent him over there" she remembers. Looking back, it is the one thing she would have stopped doing earlier than she did: "I didn't have to insert myself as much as I did. I could have been more accepting of their parenting style and taken [Kim's] feelings into consideration a little more."

Sheree suggested that we as mothers adjust our expectations: "Nobody is going to measure up to my standards of loving my son. I already know that. They can love them well. They can love them differently. But it is just impossible for anybody else to love your baby like you. So have realistic expectations."

Even as you look at adjusting your expectations, you also must accept that you are not the better parent simply because you are the mother. Our culture tells us this, but it's just not true. Emma Johnson holds book groups with thousands of single moms and remembers one woman who shared with the group that her ex and his new girlfriend were moving in together. Emma recalled that "she wanted to inspect the house before she let her daughter go over there." In Emma's opinion, this is an absurd request: "No one would think it's fair for the ex to come into the house to be sure the sheets match the comforter." These rules—inspections and the divorce decrees that stipulate how much time must pass before a parent can introduce a new partner to their children—are about control. It's an attempt to have a say in what happens in this house. It is disrespecting a healthy boundary. "If you suspect that your child is being abused, then step in, call the police. Otherwise, inserting myself into their situation is only a way to make myself feel important. It's not necessary."

Observing boundaries works both ways. Wendy had this insight for women developing a relationship with their partner's children, advice that she heard on a radio program many years earlier: "Remember, as a stepparent, you are primarily a host. You are not a parent. Your job is to make sure that the kids have a good time and that they are comfortable and well cared for. You shouldn't try to be a parent. That doesn't mean you don't give advice or guidance. That doesn't mean that you let them run roughshod all over you. They are in your home, and you are in control of the situation. You're the adult. But don't try to be their mother. They have a mother." Today, she is very close to her adult stepsons—who ultimately came to consider her a maternal figure—and believes that being mindful that her role was essentially a supportive one (supportive of her husband and deferential to her stepsons' mother, Joyce) really helped smooth the path for her bond with Joyce.

THE BLUEPRINT IN ACTION

When Kasseem entered first grade, we decided that he would be at his father's house every Thursday and Friday and then every other weekend. Swizz has never been great with keeping track of dates and times. Don't get me wrong: he always shows up, but he just needs someone to help him remember the details. He suggested that I start speaking to Alicia about schedules and visits.

At first I didn't get it. Why would he want it this way? Didn't he want to be responsible for his son's visits? These were ego-driven questions. Instead of letting myself get upset, I quickly did a self-check. Was my reaction appropriate? Was this about my son or my own feelings and insecurities? I recognized that I was building up an emotion that created a negative feeling. Ego was pushing me to believe that Swizz was detaching himself from his responsibilities to Kasseem. But that wasn't the case at all. Swizz was aware that his weakness around scheduling could cause snafus with his spending time with Kasseem, so he sought a solution to avoid that entirely. This was a good example of quickly reversing negative thoughts into positive ones. Self-work is an amazing career. It's like once you start the job, you never leave the office. I was able to set myself straight right away.

In fact, this idea of my working with Alicia on the scheduling was one of the best ideas Swizz ever had. Sharing this responsibility brought us closer together, and it also taught us how to manage ourselves as mothers. It forced us to learn each other. We better understood each other's shared values and what made us different. Most of all, we learned how to be kind and honest to each other. Who would've ever thought that creating visitation calendars together would lead to a life full of patience, love, and understanding? Well, it did. I suspect Swizz knew this would happen when he requested it. Ever wonder where Kasseem gets his slickness from?

THE FAMILY THAT SPENDS TIME TOGETHER WILL EVOLVE TOGETHER

Since that epic sixth birthday party, there's been a consistent flow of communication among Alicia, myself, and Swizz on Kasseem's behalf by text and email. But nothing replaces face-to-face interaction. Alicia and I will have a Mommy lunch, or the three of us will gather at one of our homes and just talk about life generally. Our relationships with one another need to be nurtured in order for us to be effective co-parents.

It is also very important that we plan something together as a family at least once every two months. On a Sunday, we might play family games followed by lunch or dinner. This helps give our children a sense of unity in their family.

At one point, we even shared a family pet. A bunny that Kasseem named Bella that we agreed would travel with him from one home to the next. Yes, a blending bunny. Having a shared pet was a great learning tool for Kasseem; he was able to see firsthand what his own life looked like from the perspective of an animal. The bunny had a double set of everything: two beds, two toys, two separate lives all tied together by the same people, just like Kasseem. I'll admit, it was a lot of work. Alicia and I constantly asked ourselves, "What the heck did we get ourselves into!" But it helped us through a tough patch with Kasseem. He wanted a pet, and the bunny gave him something that was his own within our family dynamic.

THE FAMILY MEETING

In her book *If I Have to Tell You One More Time . . .* , parenting expert Amy McCready suggests that every family have weekly meetings during which parents and children can review calendars, make decisions together, and do something fun. For blending families, it's also an excellent idea to have a regularly scheduled meeting (perhaps every six weeks) that includes all co-parents and siblings. During that meeting, you can review the visitation schedules and make big decisions, such as how to celebrate holidays, what to do on vacation, or whether to get a family pet. These meetings can begin with compliments and appreciations for each member, reinforcing a feeling of connectedness. It provides a natural setting for reevaluating norms and practices and resolving conflicts or behavioral problems.

We adopted family meetings very early on. When Kasseem turned seven years old, he began showing signs of displacement and sadness and had started to act out in school. My blenders and I were in a good place; we were communicating well and feeling positively about our parenting partnership, but one main ingredient was missing. We still hadn't exposed our true energy to one another yet. It was time to sit down together for a family meeting.

I sent out the request, and it was quickly accepted with a dinner invite to their home. We sat around the living room, talked, and played with the kids in order to get them acclimated to this new dynamic of Kasseem's mom being present in the home. Then we went upstairs to a private room and opened the floor to conversation. I brought up the questions that Kasseem had about our relationships and my belief that he was picking up on whatever energy or confusion toward one another that lingered. The three of us agreed that we wanted to change his mind about this. I suggested that we start spending more time together in his presence. Alicia quickly suggested that we should aim to have a family meeting once a month.

After the adults discussed everything, we invited Kasseem into the room to share his feelings. This was key to our meeting because it was important for Kasseem to witness us coming together for his well-being. Kasseem spoke his seven-year-old truth, and we all responded directly to him, individually and collectively. He said he would like to spend more time with us all as a family. He wanted me to come visit Dad's house and for Dad and Umi to come visit my house, and he wanted us to see his bedroom in both places. The adults agreed to all these things.

This conversation was a full-circle moment. Would we have been ready to sit in one another's presence three years prior? I doubt it. We needed to grow. I was overwhelmed by a feeling of relief. For the first time, I knew deep in my heart that I would no longer feel like I was raising a child on my own. This was the moment our blended evolution became real. We all came to the realization that we were in fact playing on the same team, for the same win—our son.

After this first meeting, we developed a few key strategies for problem solving within our blended family.

1. We always meet in a mutually comfortable place.
2. We make a point of sharing with one another all the good things happening in our family before tackling the things that require change or adjustment.
3. We listen to all viewpoints even if we don't agree.
4. We make sure we all feel valued and emotionally safe in one another's presence.
5. We are always mindful of our tone and energy.
6. We never leave a meeting upset.
7. We keep the focus of the conversation on the child.
8. We open each meeting with prayer, set intentions from a place of light and love, and close each meeting with a prayer.

It is important that family meetings are reserved not only for when there is a problem. According to McCready, it's best if the meetings become a regular part of a blended family's routine. Children need practice identifying and articulating their needs to adults. Our family has reached a place so steady, so solid, that Kasseem is at ease with asking us things about his two homes, the settings and rules openly, in the presence of all of us. He holds no secrets and doesn't worry about offending the parent he's not with at the time. The consistency of these meetings has led us to this safe place for our child.

CONSENSUS

The family meeting is also essential for developing consensus, which is essential for family harmony. McCready points out that when families use a "majority wins" approach, there are winners and losers. With consensus, the outcome may not be what one parent or child particularly wanted, but it is something everyone can live with. Consensus is not always easy. It's something all people must work toward developing. However, it is one of the most important things parents can do to give their kids a stable, supportive atmosphere.

We decide how to spend birthdays and holidays and how to split vacation time through consensus. For summer vacation, we usually set up an every-two-weeks visiting schedule in June and July. Then by mid-July until September we do an every-other-week visit. For Thanksgiving and Christmas, Kasseem usually spends the early half of the day with me and then we go to his father's house and hang out together for a while, or vice versa. On his birthday, sometimes we have one big party, other times separate small parties or family dinners where everyone is welcomed. No matter how you put it, we've reached a point where the invitation is always open. Seriously, always! I know that's hard to believe because co-parents never imagine this level of coexisting for themselves, but it's possible, and it can be you. It's by far the most rewarding gift any co-parent can ask for.

Since that epic sixth birthday party, there's been a consistent flow of communication among Alicia, myself, and Swizz. Here we are celebrating Kasseem's eighth birthday.

We decide how to spend birthdays and holidays and how to split vacation time through consensus. On Kasseem's birthday, sometimes we have one big party, other times separate small parties or family dinners where everyone is welcomed. We've reached a point where the invitation is always open.

Kasseem's ninth birthday party.

Here we are sitting around the Thanksgiving table in 2013. I'm sitting between Swizz and Alicia, with Kasseem on my lap.

Thanksgiving 2017. It may be hard to believe this level of coexistence. But it is possible, and it can be you.

BRINGING IN SOMEONE NEW

People are always asking me, "Mashonda, when are you going to find new love for yourself?" In fact, I have dated a few amazing men over the past eight years. From 2015 to 2016, I had my first serious relationship since my divorce. I was always very picky about who I brought around my son. I never wanted to expose him to anything that wasn't real, so until that time, Kasseem never knew of his mommy having a boyfriend. Before there were any introductions (to Kasseem and my co-parents), I laid out everything for him. This man was made to understand that my son is the most important thing in my life, and he had to be willing to make Kasseem an important part of his life. I explained to him at the beginning of our relationship what type of family he was getting into. "We are not a normal co-parenting family," I told him. "We all actually get along and coexist. So if you're going to be a part of my life and Kasseem's life, you will have to be a part of our blend."

The guy spent a lot of time with Kasseem, met with Swizz and Alicia, and we all got along. We even had family meetings about Kasseem's development and created ways that we could all play proactive roles in his life. It was a great experience for Kasseem to witness a man in my life on that level. Even though our relationship didn't work out, I am grateful that it was with someone who was understanding and willing to consciously parent with me.

Misa believes that dating could be a part of the healing process for a woman: "You're going to fall and bruise yourself and bump around a little bit, but it will give you some experience, some confidence. It gives you some room to see what life is like in a new way, and companionship is important. Dates are harmless. Go on out to dinner, get drinks, dancing, a little travel. Whatever you're comfortable with. Every girl needs to have some fun!" But she warns women to make sure they be clear about what they want and what they're ready for.

Sheree advises that as a woman and a mother, you should avoid bringing unresolved issues into a new situation. It's tempting to rush into somebody's arms. "We just want the love and affection." But if you haven't made complete peace with the last situation and allowed yourself to fully understand what happened, you'd be making a mistake.

For me, the ideal relationship starts with my relationship to myself. It's only when you become a fully conscious woman that you know what to truly look for in a partner. I could only be with a man who has already put time and effort into his own self-work. His ego and emotions must be under control. Malik Yoba agrees with this: "I've been the guy on the first date who will say, 'Okay. Let's talk about trauma and what you have gone through.' I'd bring this up just to see how they would respond. If they were like, 'Ah, I can't get that deep,' I know I can't really mess with her."

Sheree advised that you should look for someone who has integrity, someone who does what they say they are going to do and says what they mean, "somebody with stability." Patience and kindness are also important. This person will be around your child and should exhibit qualities you want your child to emulate.

Dating someone who doesn't have children can be extra complicated. Sometimes you will find that partners who don't have children
won't fully understand your drive to go above and beyond for your
child's long-term emotional success. It's important to be with someone who isn't judgmental or overly critical about your parenting
choices.

He also can't be threatened by the relationship you have built
with your ex or the dedication that you feel toward your child. He
must be open enough to have communication with my blenders and
have an open place in his heart for our family dynamic. The person
needs to develop a good balance in your blend and be comfortable
there.

For some people, my list of must-haves might be long. True love
will come my way when it is time. I'm not concerned. Granny Sandra
told me, "Let God send him to you. When we look, we tend to pick
the wrong guy. God knows the what, when, and who, because He
knows our needs."

In the meantime, I believe that people need to work on themselves before they pull others so deeply into their worlds. I had a lot
of cleaning up to do in my life, a lot of self-repair. I focused my energy
on what mattered most: me and my son.

The Divine Blueprint is how the adults work with one another in
order to create an environment for their children. In the next chapter, I'll speak to how we connect to the children in our midst, which
truly is the most important part of it all.

CHAPTER 9

The Nucleus Child

Parenting expert Amy McCready borrows the term "family constellation" from Adlerian psychology to frame a way of understanding a child's behavior. The family constellation describes the makeup of a family—who belongs to the family unit and how they interact with one another. Children have two basic emotional, subconscious needs: one is a sense of personal power or control over their present and future. The other is a sense of belonging, which is the feeling of being emotionally connected to the adults who take care of them and the degree to which they feel secure within the family constellation.

Indeed, the makeup of the family constellation is subject to change. For example, when a new sibling joins the family, there is a shift in everyone's role in order to incorporate the new member. An older child might feel "dethroned" from his "place" within the family and will act out with negative behavior to restore the attention and power he is accustomed to having all to himself.

A divorce or separation completely rocks the original constellation for everyone involved. Now instead of one constellation—two parents and their shared child—there is an extreme redesign: two separate constellations representing two different homes.

When parents separate, children are confronted with the reality that they have no control over their parents' relationship. The expectation that they will see both parents every day is also no longer valid. These things can make a child feel particularly powerless. And now there is the additional task of finding out how one is supposed to fit into two new family constellations, especially if one or both parents enter into new relationships and have more children. It's no surprise that kids in this situation act out and engage in power struggles. Feeling uncertain about where they belong and how they are significant to the adults around them, they tend to seek belonging and significance in negative ways.

In her work with families, McCready recognized that children were misbehaving in ways that were directly related to separation and divorce—especially if they were shuttled back and forth between their parents' homes. When Sara separated from her husband, their son, Ethan, was eight years old. In the first few months of going back and forth between his dad's home and Sara's new apartment, Ethan flatly refused to do simple things like brush his teeth in the morning or put on his shoes when it was time to go to school. This is very typical. A child might suddenly become resistant to executing everyday routines or suddenly act helpless in areas in which she is perfectly capable. After repeatedly asking her son why he was misbehaving, Ethan looked his mother in the eyes and told her that he would continue to misbehave until she "came back home." For Sara, this was a revelation. Her son had been trying to communicate his helplessness and frustration about the divorce in the only way he knew how—by causing disruption to the daily routine.

Some children will play one parent against the other, using guilt, the threat of a tantrum, or any other negative behavior to manipulate the parent to get what he wants. These and other similar negative habits have one thing in common: the child's attempt to grab back the power she feels she has lost.

We have to remember that children in blended families have a lot on their plate. Their situation is not traditional, and they can't relate to their best friend, who still has a mother and a father living under the same roof. Sometimes this reality takes a toll on them, and there's not much we as parents can say to make them feel better. We have to give them a safe, guided space to get through their emotions in these times. This is another example of empathy, patience, and understanding.

Instead of getting upset at our children when they act out or show signs of frustration that end up making our egos feel disrespected, once in a while, let's slip into their small shoes and imagine what it's like to be a human who has no say over his existence yet still has to manage his own energy and all the extra new energies that have been introduced into his life.

ANCHORING THE CHILD

Children with separated parents often feel untethered: not quite sure of where they belong or how they are significant to the adults around them. The work of blending a family is to bring the two new family constellations closer together so they overlap. Instead of the child being in the emotionally precarious position of being transferred from one separated constellation to the other, the overlapping constellations create a stable, secure center—a nucleus—where the shared child can more comfortably exist. In our family, the nucleus child is Kasseem. In this position, his sense of security and belonging is repeatedly reinforced by family meetings, by one-on-one time with all the adults in his life, and by contributing to whichever household he is in.

In pulling the constellations toward each other, we are not painting the homes with the same color. It's important to maintain the integrity of each home—keeping the mini constellations intact within the larger framework. Kasseem and I have our own family meetings and our own set of rules and expectations that are specific to our home.

In her book, *What Great Parents Do*, Erica Reischer describes the three key principles—or ABCs—of great parenting: Acceptance, Boundaries, and Consistency. These are all important, but I want you to zero in on the principle of Consistency. Consistency means that you do what you say you will do every time. For children who have come through a reconfiguration of their family, it is important for

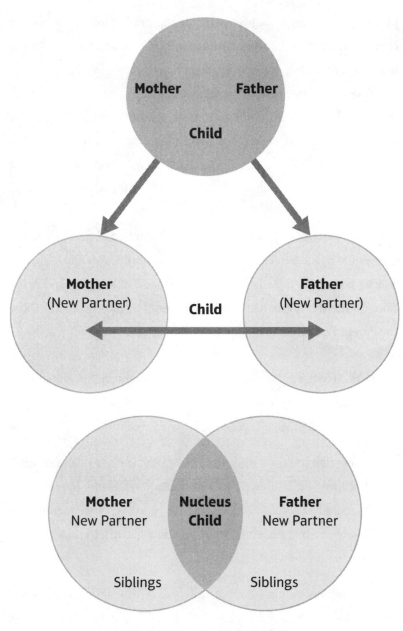

BLENDED FAMILY

parents to recommit themselves to being predictable. It's a way of rebuilding trust and respect, anchoring your children in patterns that make them feel secure.

When Kasseem returns to my home after a visit with his father, we have what's called "so, what's new?" conversations. We discuss what we each experienced while apart and describe how we're feeling in that moment. We may go sit in a park, go for a run, or simply just hug it out for a while, but we always take that time to reconnect and settle in.

Since there is no drama with my co-parents, I actually have the energy and peace to really tune in to how my child is feeling. If a child is acting out, it's usually because they need one of the following things: Attention, Connection, Affirmation, or a Reset. I call these the Parent Buttons.

If it's **Attention** the child needs, then a parent should get actively involved. Give the child some one-on-one time, even if it's just a quick board game or a relaxing walk around the block.

Connection usually calls for higher involvement: a hug, a whisper of "I love you so much." Meditation always works for me here. Kasseem has gotten to a point where he asks that we meditate or pray before bed some nights. When he does this, I know that he's had a pretty demanding day.

Affirmation. Adults automatically feel as though we're supposed to have the bigger voice. We're inclined to believe that things should go "our way or no way." However, "our way" is solely based on our experiences. Our children must walk their own path, and we must find the balance that allows them free will and protection. Just because our children are smaller than us in size doesn't mean that their spirits aren't as big as ours. As grown-ups, we don't always have to be right about everything, nor should we ever make their voice and opinions feel small. Let them win the debate sometimes. This is an affirmation for their spirits and gives us grown-ups an opportunity to practice vulnerability and tame our own egos.

As an adult woman, I know what it's like to just want to shut down every so often. It doesn't mean that I'm upset or indifferent; it just means that I need a **Reset**—some time alone to decompress from whatever life has thrown my way. Don't think for one moment that your child isn't sometimes overwhelmed by life. Encourage a nap or some time alone. Many times when Kasseem has an attitude it's because he needs to do some inner work, ground himself, or realign his energy. Monitoring and adjusting one's energy independently is something we practice in both homes.

MIND, BODY, SOUL TIME

My Parent Buttons are very similar to what parenting expert Amy McCready describes as Mind, Body, Soul Time. Each parent (both bonus and biological) is encouraged to schedule ten to fifteen minutes every day of one-on-one time with no interruptions, during which the child gets to decide the activity. Family meetings build the cohesiveness of the family unit and allow a child to assert her role in the family. Mind, Body, Soul Time strengthens the bonds between child and adult and is ideal for warding off misbehavior.

There is a tendency to use these ten minutes to ask the child questions like, "Well, how did school go today? How did you do on your math test? How was soccer practice?" The MBST is then reduced to a drill of how the day went (imagine this line of questioning with each adult in your child's life); Instead Mind, Body and Soul Time requires questions like "What would be the most fun thing for us to do together in these ten minutes?" Perhaps it is building LEGOs, a quick game of Uno, even pulling together the ingredients for a cake. So much of a child's day is adult-directed. There is a grown-up who determines when it's time to eat, when it's time for math class, when it's time to do your homework, etc. Mind, Body, Soul Time gives the child a chance to call the shots.

For the days that the child is not in your home, you can have MBST on the phone, via Skype, or by FaceTime. It could even be a part of the bedtime routine. Perhaps your child can decide what book you're going to read together or what song you're going to sing.

Being consistent about this time and even labeling it is important. Kasseem and I have Mommy and Son time, Swizz and Kasseem have man-to-man talk, and Alicia and Kasseem have Umi/KJ time. Afterward, each parent could say, "I really enjoy our Mommy and Son time." For the child, the message reinforced is "I am so significant that she carves out this time to spend with just me."

FAMILY CONTRIBUTIONS

Another way of grounding a child's sense of belonging is by initiating what McCready calls Family Contributions—tasks that your child is expected to complete in the home, whether she lives there part-time or full-time. Unloading the dishwasher can be looked upon as a dreaded chore, but it takes on a different energy if the child understands that the task is necessary for the family to work effectively. You can't sit and have dinner together if the dishes are all in the dishwasher.

At my house, Kasseem does the laundry and takes out the garbage. At his dad's house, he takes care of the family dog and washes dishes. When everybody in the family contributes, their role in the home is more defined and their sense of belonging is boosted. Family Contributions have the added benefit of helping a child acquire and accomplish new skills, which is a self-esteem builder. It's key for the child to have Family Contributions in both homes and for the parents to communicate about them. This removes the possibility that a child will use the existence of household tasks in one home and not the other to pit one parent against the other.

One thing I would include in this category of Family Contributions is most definitely responsibility for personal belongings. Every co-parent can describe at least one scenario wherein a child was sent for a visit or returned back home with new clothing, a new haircut, and a bag full of new toys only for the child to be returned looking messy with several pieces of clothing missing. Simple, silly things like this have the power to set an awkward, upsetting tone in any family dynamic. Let's avoid these moments from even existing. Teach your child to respect his or her belongings and the belongings of others. If he has a favorite sweater, he knows it's his favorite sweater, so he should make sure it accompanies him from house to house.

> **"When my daughter goes to spend time with her father, I pack her clothes, make sure her hair is clean and neat, and include written instructions for her homework. She returns home looking a mess with half of her clothing missing. This is driving me crazy! What are they doing over there?"**
>
> When a child shares two homes, things will get misplaced or forgotten once in a while. This is a fact. And realistically, everyone's idea of what neat hair is supposed to look like will vary. The sooner you accept these things, the sooner the stress of it all will fade away.
>
> It's a must that we go the extra mile to teach our children at an early age to be responsible for and respectful of their belongings. In the past four years, my son has forgotten at his dad's house new sneakers or school clothes that I purchased, but he also ends up with their stuff at my house too.
>
> If your child is underage and can't take care of herself, the only thing you have left to lean on is communication with your co-parent. A simple text or note in a bookbag: "Hope your visit goes well, please return the blue sweatshirt. Thanks."

Kasseem is now old enough to pack his bag the night before he is returned to our home (albeit with a lot of reminders). He knows what he needs in both settings and which parents want to see him with items they personally purchased. Taking control over their belongings is something that we literally must begin to drill into our children's minds before they reach adolescence or else they will always become adults who are mindless about their personal property.

I find it useful to always send a text the day before Kasseem arrives at his dad's house with a list of what needs to be returned. If there's homework that needs to be discussed or reviewed, I also include that in a note or simply forward directly over to Alicia whatever details his teacher might send.

When things go awry during the transition between homes, don't go "crazy." Fall back on self-control and proper conduct in order to achieve a winning outcome. Pull in some patience and kindness, not only to your child but also to your blenders. It takes time and consistency on the parents' part to make sure the child understands how important returning items are. Sometimes it takes equal time for the parents to grasp and respect this as well. You'll get there.

TWO HOMES, ONE TEAM

One might think that it is confusing for a child to manage two different family constellations. But in fact, children are very adaptable. Kasseem is extremely sensitive to the distinctions between our house and his dad's house. At my house he is the only child and he gets all the love and attention. He feels like the king. When he is at his father's house, he has a new role, that of a big brother to two younger siblings. Sometimes this drives him crazy because he would rather be the king of the house, not just one of the princes. Growing up with siblings is a gift that I haven't been able to provide him with yet. Being immersed in all the masculine energy in that home is something I can't provide. However, I'm sure that the differences in both homes are helping to make Kasseem a well rounded adult.

Your child is also very capable of following different rules at different houses. As parents, we have to be vigilant about being consistent with our own rules. You are your child's parent, and it's your job to decide what is in the best interest of that child when he is in your home. And then stick to those rules. Again, consistency is the secret ingredient here.

I've noticed that children have a way of managing their own emotions (whether it be stress or sadness) by using manipulation as a tool. Adults have to be very mindful of this and check their children right away. We can't allow ourselves to fall for this manipulation. When you and your co-parents are working together and communicating, the divide-and-conquer tactic never makes it to your child's arsenal. Establish rules and expectations in your home and follow through on the established consequences for not matching those expectations. Being consistent in your own home is essential. Supporting your co-parents' rules in their home is equally vital. If you join your child in bemoaning the rules at his other parent's house, you're showing a crack in the united front, and the consequences will be visited upon you in your home.

Here's an example from our lives. At my house, Kasseem is allowed to stay up until 9:00 p.m. At Alicia and Swizz's house, he has two younger brothers, which makes an earlier bedtime necessary. Kasseem isn't thrilled about this and has called to complain to me about it on numerous occasions. But rather than intervene on his behalf, I maintain my position as teammate and explain to him that at his dad's house, the bedtime is what they choose. We must show positive reinforcement in situations like this. Children will try to match our energy. If we seem annoyed or disturbed about a co-parent's decision, don't display those feelings in front of your child. Save it for an adult conversation.

Sheree and Will also had a complete team approach when raising Trey, with Jada as essential support. Sheree said, "At the end of the day, I wanted my son to feel safe and secure, to feel as though he's loved by both parents. Will is an extension of my son, and as such, I need to cover him. That's my obligation. We can be living in different cities, different countries. We're still a team when it comes to our son. And my son has to know that." Although the three adults may have had different approaches to child-rearing, they were on the same page when it came to Trey. There were rules that applied "across the board." That was important, because it "created less confusion and fewer loopholes" for Trey. Truthfully, this is easier when the child is young. It becomes more complicated as the children grow older and face more complex issues. But even then, communication and respect are key.

THE NONNEGOTIABLES

Part of maintaining teamwork is coming to a consensus over the nonnegotiables. Nonnegotiables are those values and expectations that both homes share. There should not be a ton of these—just a few that relate to a child's overall development. Alicia, Swizz, and I share certain rules about Kasseem's schoolwork, diet, cell phone usage, and which types of media (music and television) he can be exposed to. Erica Reischer advises that "less is more" when it comes to rules. You want only as many rules as you know everyone is committed to enforcing consistently. Establishing the nonnegotiables really helps co-parents become more purposeful about their parenting goals and style.

According to Amy McCready, parents should balance the nonnegotiables with giving kids plenty of opportunity to make choices. "Getting the child involved in menu planning for the week, or we're going to go out to dinner on Friday night and we can spend twenty-five dollars. Let's figure out where you want to go. We can't let them call the shots on everything. But if parents are too militant about making every decision, the kids will seek to exert power in other ways."

TURNING POINTS

Children are especially dynamic creatures, always evolving and growing and adjusting. Even with instruments such as family meetings and MBST, parents might face a challenge from their kids around the routine. For us, this happened when Kasseem was eleven. We had been blending for more than five years, with Kasseem spending almost equal amounts of time between my home and his father's. But in the summer, something new had developed, and as parents, we just couldn't wrap our heads around it. Kasseem said to me, "I don't want to have two homes sometimes. I wish I didn't have to leave you." I didn't look at this statement as a negative. It just assured me that he was paying attention to his surroundings and was able to express himself emotionally. That's a good thing. However, he fell into a stage of extreme discomfort. He was angry all the time and clearly struggling with his emotions. He told me that he felt his younger brother Egypt received all the attention, and it was causing him to feel as though there was no advocate for him at his dad's house.

It was time for a family meeting. Alicia and I discussed it on the phone first. We knew how important this meeting was and wanted to be prepared with notes and bullet points. We decided that it was best to have three meetings: one with just the adults, another with the adults and Kasseem, and the third with Egypt involved.

Our overall goal was to understand exactly where Kasseem's anger stemmed from and then help him express how we could fix this.

We knew that Egypt had a role to play as the little brother, and there was some classic sibling rivalry involved. We also knew that Kasseem was playing off the fact that he is my only child at home and gets all the attention in my home but then has to share this attention at his dad's house.

At the adults-only meeting, we agreed that it was very important that Kasseem understand that he was free to express himself and that his feelings would be supported. When he joined us, we made a conscious effort to first acknowledge all the magnificent things he'd been doing before we delved into the issues. We wanted him to be open and willing to share his thoughts. And he certainly did. He said he felt neglected when he was at his dad's house. He complained that everyone listened to Egypt more than him. Alicia and Swizz knew this wasn't how they saw things, but they never made Kasseem feel wrong for expressing himself; they simply heard him out without allowing ego to take over.

After Kasseem spoke, Swizz chimed in. He related to Kasseem's struggle because he himself is the oldest of five brothers and realized the peace in the house was being disrupted by the brothers disrespecting each other's space and personal boundaries. While we all recognized that Egypt was younger and wanted to always be around his big brother, whom he admires, we can also relate to being older and just not wanting to be bothered or forced into playing if we really didn't want to. We explained to Kasseem that he had to learn patience with his little brother and also think of different ways to deal with him instead of showing him that he was fed up or aggravated.

After our talk with Kasseem, I could feel the weight lifted from him. He felt loved and supported by his parents. That is all any child ever yearns for.

Swizz, Alicia, and I decided right then that it was important that Swizz and Alicia start to spend more solo time with Kasseem. We also began to think of new ways to help him quickly identify with and communicate his feelings instead of allowing them to build up to a boiling point. Kasseem has always enjoyed guided meditation, stretching, and massages, so we started doing those more often. Swizz started spending more time with Kasseem alone during his time at the house, even taking him to the recording studio. Alicia also suggested taking him on trips with her alone, taking him on walks, and spending extra time at night reading to him. We knew what we had to do and were ready to make the changes.

Later, Swizz had a private conversation with Egypt about how important it was to have your brother's back, no matter what. He encouraged Egypt to always find a way to work things out with Kasseem, without the boys trying to get each other in trouble. "Sometimes Kasseem won't want to play with you; you have to respect his decision," Swizz told Egypt.

Months after this meeting, I still asked Kasseem how everything was going at his dad's house with Egypt. "Things are much better, Mom. I know how to deal with my feelings now, and I know how to deal with my little brother," he said.

Dear older version of myself,

Here's what I want you to know about your younger years as a child in a blended family.

My mom asked me to write this letter for her book, a letter to my older self, as a man. I'm still not sure what this means but she said one day I will thank her.

When I was six years old, all I wanted was to understand why my mom and dad didn't live together or why everything felt sad when they were around each other. Even though I was just a little kid, I felt worried, wondering if they would speak kindly to one another or even just smile. I didn't like how it felt to not spend time with both parents but when we were all together something just didn't feel right. This made me confused.

I felt very different from my other friends, and I worried they would judge me because my family was different than theirs. Most of my peers lived at home with both parents. I didn't like traveling back and forth between houses. All of it made me feel out of place.

What helped a little bit was knowing that I wasn't the only one with a blended family. My best friend from first to fifth grade had one too, and we spent a lot of time together comparing our experiences. Neither of us really understood the way our families were set up; we just knew that it was our life and it was different from other kids at school. Most of the time we played together and did things to distract ourselves from our realities. But, we shared many of the same challenges like having to leave our moms' houses at times when we weren't ready to do so, or not being able to do things at our moms' houses that we could do at our dads' houses. We also both could relate to the worry that comes when you have pick a parent to do certain things with and maybe hurt the other parent's feelings. Sharing these situations with another kid made both my best friend and me feel better.

As I got older (now I'm eleven), I felt more secure. When my parents started to work as a team, everything got easier. Mom, Dad, and Umi started having meetings for all of us to talk together. I felt like we were on a team. All along, I just wanted my parents to be friends. It made me feel normal.

Having a good, consistent schedule (one that I can remember and know won't change abruptly), having co-parents that like each other, and everyone learning to be patient with one another and show respect are the things I think have helped us become a better family. My advice to children in blended families is don't give up on your parents; remember they love you and may not realize what you're going through. Try your best to explain your feelings to them.

My advice to the parents is this: remember that we are just kids and we need to be surrounded by peace and love. Stay strong and make smart decisions for your kids because you are all we really have.

Sincerely,

Kasseem Jr.

THE BLESSING OF SIBLINGS

My son, Kasseem, has three brothers and a sister. These four people have added immeasurably to his life. One of the biggest bonuses of a blended family is the ability to develop a free, full relationship with your siblings. Siblings also present a unique challenge, and that is sibling rivalry.

It's almost inevitable that siblings will be in competition with one another—often for their parent's attention or acceptance. Most kids don't realize that their anger at a sister or brother stems from jealousy because she is "the athletic one" or because the baby seems to take up all of Dad's time. The perception of favoritism is dangerous because children don't always see clearly what's real or what's not.

Although sibling rivalry happens in every family, it is increased in families in which everyone does not have the same parents and children don't live together full time. Parenting expert Amy Mc-Cready gives excellent advice on warding off sibling rivalry in a blended family.

1. The adults in the home should spend Mind, Body, and Soul Time with each child every day. This helps kids see that they're valued individually.
2. Encourage siblings to have Mind, Body, and Soul Time with one another.
3. Establish a policy around how family members should speak to one another. Discuss which words are unkind and what type of communication is verbally abusive.
4. Take the time to train your children to resolve conflicts. We tend to get frustrated with our kids because they can't work out disagreements with one another. In fact, conflict resolution is an advanced skill that many adults haven't mastered. Make sure that your children are able to listen well and apply good com-

munication and problem-solving skills. After you've given them the tools, let them know you expect them to solve their own conflicts. If they come to you with a conflict, ask them, "What have you done to try to solve that problem?" And then stay out of it, even if you need to leave the room and listen at a distance. Only intervene if the children step outside already established norms for communication.

5. Be careful not to create unnecessary competition, such as who can get upstairs and get dressed the fastest or who can be the first into the car. This only serves to raise the stress level in the home and promote competition in other areas of life—not exactly what you're going for in a blended family!

6. Reduce all labeling! Resist describing your children as "the athletic one" or "the smart one" or "the clown." Even words like "stepson" or "half sister" can create division. Your children are simply that: "our children."

NO HALF-SIBLINGS

Kasseem and his brother Egypt.

Kasseem and his brother Genesis.

When interviewing several blended families, I discovered one common thing: no one used the term "half-sibling."

Sheree never refers to Trey's brother and sister as his half-siblings. She remembers taking Trey to the orthodontist, and the receptionist asked him, "How is your half brother?" and Trey looked at her completely confused. "What does 'half-sibling' really mean? Yes, Trey knows his brother and sister have a different mother. But what does it really imply? Jada, Will, and I always wanted to facilitate a closeness between the siblings. The child should always be separate from parents. Every baby is a new little being. We shouldn't attach anything extra to them because of how they came into the world. I remember when Jaden was born. He was just one of the cutest babies you would ever want to see. Absolutely juicy adorable and so sweet. He called Trey 'Brah Brah.' Jaden would come and stay with me, and I welcomed him. I loved having him in my home. We were always inclusive. You can't always be together when you're living in two separate households and have separate lives. But if there was ever something to do with the kids, we all came together as one family."

Misa's son has four siblings, and she's especially proud that they are all so close: "Perhaps in the early years, we hit a few learning curves and could have handled things better. But we were always able to keep our issues away from the kids. And the siblings' relationships with one another is super healthy as a result. I see how much they love each other, how much they support each other. It's a blessing."

Part of how she fortified the bond between her son and his siblings was showing Justin how much she cared about them. "I wanted him to know that I loved his brother [Christian] as much as he did, and that I was proud of his brother's accomplishments as much as he was, and that he could share that with me and we could share that with each other. That I didn't want Justin to ever feel any separation or the need to feel like he had to keep things from me that he might be happy about or proud about or feel that if he showed love to his brother or siblings. To this day, I am very happy and proud that Christian's eyes light up when he sees me. He remembers that I was always kind to him. Kids grow up, but they always remember."

Malik Yoba was a big believer in bringing all his children to-gether as often as possible. Raising children from different moms may not have been an easy task, but it was his "deliberate intention" that they have summers, holidays, and school vacations together starting when they were very young. He is incredibly proud of their closeness, that they consider one another best friends. "The most im-portant thing was to stay consistent and do whatever you can to make sure they spend time together. Then this togetherness becomes the life that they know."

Wendy's bonus and biological children are extremely close. Her daughters are in their twenties, and her stepsons are in their late thirties, with wives and children of their own. They all talk and text at least once a day and spend weekends with one another. "If a person ever described them as 'half-siblings,' I'm sure they would get pissed off." From the time the girls were born, their preteen siblings em-braced them: "With my older daughter, they stayed back from camp in order to be there when she was born. I have tons of photographs with them holding their sisters, playing with their sisters. Now we have similar pictures with the girls and their nieces and nephews." If she is forced to ponder how she fostered this closeness, Wendy says, "I can't say that I ever consciously did anything, except that I loved the boys so genuinely and made them a part of my life so genuinely that there was never any sense of 'this one's mine, this one's yours.' They were just one big team of siblings."

Taraqa, who gained four siblings when his father remarried, always makes a point of incorporating his siblings into his life. This is for his children's sake, as well as his own. "I think the question to keep trying to engage is how do we get a little more access to who we are? How are we going to find peace with who we are? That process includes your siblings, your parents, your grandparents. Being with them, talking with them, helps you see how their thoughts and actions are your own and how your interpretations of what they said or did helped shape you."

Blending is not only important for the nucleus child but for all the children involved. It will protect their mental health, their emotional stability, and their willingness to connect with those who will love them unconditionally. Siblings serve as a direct reminder of our own individual connection to the Divine. They are not only carriers of our same blood or proof of scientific DNA. Their complete existence is a reminder of our very own nature and beginnings on Earth. This is something rare, something worth valuing. And this means more than anything.

THE VICTORY OF PEACE

Blending isn't all family vacations and joint holiday dinners. It's more than just happy photos of dancing kids and hugging parents with trending hashtags for Instagram. Blending is real life, real emotions, interactions, and circumstances. It's an ongoing project that becomes a lifestyle. There are moments of joy and bliss and times when our balance is tested. Because we're human. My family isn't perfect; we are and will constantly be a work in progress.

Much of this work has to do with tempering ego. And that is a tremendous challenge. Michelle admitted that she was raised to take care of her business by any means necessary and to not complain. Just get it done. "This actually takes a lot of ego and not putting feelings aside. You react based on feelings of being disrespected. An eye for an eye. My struggle with that innate, natural reaction is my greatest and most difficult lesson yet."

Misa warns us about the danger of the ego. "It just introduces chaos and unnecessary low-vibration energy." She wants us all to realize that "when you are not coming with your best, you're not going to receive your best from others." When there is something you and your co-parents don't agree on, take three steps back and ask yourself, "Am I operating from my ego? What is this really about?" Then recognize, as Misa says, that we are all human, we are all evolving, and believe that we are doing the best we can while choosing to live our lives and raise our families.

Blending your family is a powerful demonstration of living your best life. However, it's impossible to achieve if everyone's not on the same page. If your child's other parent and/or new girlfriend/boyfriend wants nothing to do with blending, it's not your place to force them. Furthermore, it shouldn't even be your desire to try to figure out why. You need to save your energy for the things that really matter—yourself and your child.

In a situation like this, tighten up your superhero cape because you're going to have to be extra resilient. Always put your best foot forward, and never let your child know that you are affected by someone else's decisions. Learn how to compartmentalize, creating in your mind a waffle-shaped box in which everything and everyone has its space. Don't let things flow into one another. This will make your thinking very clear.

It's important to choose not to react to everything. If you feel ruffled by an action or a comment, don't jump to react. Examine your own feelings first. What's at play here? Are you really seeing things clearly, from another's perspective? Or is your ego the filter? Once you've figured these out, then you can communicate clearly.

Seek out a mediator—either a family member both of you trust or a professional—who can help create a healthy balance in your family when it comes to making major decisions. Have open conversations with your child to reassure them that they are doing the best that they can and so are you. Children grow up and remember everything their parents said and how we made them feel. Always protect your child's energy, and cradle their heart in the palms of your hands.

As I reflect on my life, I realize how truly blessed I am. Early one winter morning in 2016 I eagerly awoke from a deep slumber to start my writing assignments for this book. I sat up in a mess of pillows, sheets, and comforter intertwined under and around my body. I started to cry—the kind of crying that leaves you without breath— you feel your lungs expand and you're left blurry eyed. It wasn't a sorrowful cry. These were tears of release. I was crying because I had recognized the change from within. I had stepped into a new version of myself.

All the work I had put into restoring my spirit had completely transformed me. I was able to notice parts of myself that I had forgotten about, parts that needed to be remembered and nurtured, and parts that needed to be disposed of. I am many different women, all of whom needed love, needed light. Mashonda was blending Mashonda. It wasn't until I discovered my own personal blend that I was able to evolve into my own true self.

The Mashonda whom I am today is possible because I have found myself and I am content. I'm able to fine-tune every situation for the best possible outcome. I stay in the light that is my son's well-being, that is my mental and emotional stability. Locking in with a tunnel vision of egoless decisions keeps me in full control of myself. Gratitude pushes me forward, faith is what I breathe, and authenticity keeps me grounded.

That moment, cradled by fabric in my bed, I fully embraced a new purpose. I wanted to change the way people think about co-parenting. I wanted parents and caretakers, families, and an overall community of adults to have a new infrastructure that could create loving, safe environments for the children in their lives. My goal was to let children know that we, as adults, were focused on helping them to become healthy human beings. This would be the way I could create positive change in the world.

Not only am I the proud mother of my son, Kasseem, I also now have a beautiful blended family to share in his love, development, and overall health as a young man. As a mother, I know Kasseem's happiness is the single most important thing in my life. It took some time, but I now embrace Swizz and Alicia as my partners in this wonderful journey. It surprises me when people act as though what my co-blenders and I are doing is so unnatural and unnecessary. Some say we are doing "too much" by coexisting on the level that we do. They say, "You all don't need to be that cool; all you have to do is raise the child." I can understand why some may see things this way; everyone's level of consciousness is different, and not one single person has the ability to look into another's soul and truly see their evolution.

Here's what I know: society will make us believe that war is natural. Social media, in fact, glorifies fighting. It has become a form of modern-day entertainment, but no one really makes the headlines when they are doing the self-work, the things that improve quality of life.

There's no reason for you to stay in a box of misery and confusion even if it is easier than unfolding your wings and soaring to higher heights of love and humanity. Discord of any kind is honestly just a distraction from allowing us to experience the true meaning of life.

If I had to choose one word to describe my blended family today, it would be "flow." That's what we do best: we flow. We flow in peace.

After all has been said and done, I can't imagine not having this level of peace in my life.

My hope for you is the same.

Swizz, Alicia, and I have grown together on this journey toward blending, and it has made us better people. It was something we had to do for us and for our children. We've kept our flow private up until now but collectively decided to share our experience with the world because we know that what we've accomplished is something magical and that our testimony will help millions of families worldwide.

THE OUTRO

Dearest Kasseem,

My small hero, one day you will know how you saved my life and renewed my soul. I thank you for being my mirror, for allowing me to see the woman I desired to be through your eyes. I thank you for becoming in this lifetime an instrument of great change. You are the source that has fueled my awakening, the energy that powers my highest intentions. I thank God for you, for our connection, for the way we feel the same things. There are moments when we just lie next to each other, not one word spoken, but we feel each other's thoughts. I know this is rare and special, but it is us. No matter what life gives you, it's important that you remember your purpose, stay in your light. Love and respect everyone, especially your siblings.

They are not your halves; they are a part of what makes you whole. Always walk in that truth. The five of you are incredible children, and from the way you look at and interact with one another, I know you're going to be hand in hand for the rest of your lives. Your relationships with Nasir, Nicole, Egypt, and Genesis will live on for decades. And so, your father, Umi, and I have sought to prepare you on how and why you need to cherish one another. The set of you are our living legacy. It's our mission to teach you the tools of love.

The first time I met your brother Egypt, my heart melted. I looked at him and saw a combination of Swizz and Alicia, but I also saw you as a baby all over again. The amount of love that Egypt has in his heart for you, his big brother, is outstanding. He looks up to you and always wants to be in your presence. Egypt came equipped to add a layer of joy and experience to your life, one that I couldn't add on my own, and I am beyond grateful.

Genesis appeared four years later to bring our entire family unit even closer together. Your Umi and I spoke a lot during her pregnancy with Genesis. Our connection had gotten stronger, and by September, when Alicia was about six months pregnant, we were all in the best space that our awkward romance had ever been in. We celebrated your father's birthday that month, and soon after, for the first time, we sat at the same table for Thanksgiving dinner. We were moving as one unit, a family. Our work had paid off, and our entire family was proud of us.

A few days after you turned eight years old, Genesis was born. I'll never forget the day I first met him. He was around two weeks old, and your Umi called and said it was a great time to come meet the small prince. When I arrived, I walked into the nursery, and there he was, wrapped in a soft cotton blanket, smelling of lavender oil and at full peace in his dreams. Alicia handed him to me, then left the room to tend to Egypt. One day, you will know that a mother doesn't leave her baby with just anyone. When she walked out the door, I felt a strong sense of trust and love between us as mothers. I looked at Gen and thanked him for his safe arrival. I've had a special connection to him since that day.

I know they can be trying; younger siblings always are. But they are teaching you patience and understanding, and one day your bond will be unbreakable. And like me, you will thank them for all that they are.

Now there is also Nicole, our sweet little girl.

When I first found out that Nicole was a part of our family, I was personally going through a lot. But the news of her arrival made me slow things down to acknowledge what God had done. Nicole was born on May 22, 2008. Does that date sound familiar to you? Yes! Angel, my first son, was born on May 22, a day I will never forget, a day that used to carry only pain. I'm thankful Nicole entered the world on that date. The gift of her birth will always be a bright light among many sad memories. I love the sister she is to you. She is teaching you things about divine femininity that I can't as a mother. I love the brother you are to her—how you look at her with so much regard, how you want to protect her, how you are so gentle with her.

And there is Nasir, your big brother. I am thankful, so thankful, that Nasir always saw my true love for him as an individual, not just because he is your father's son. I thank him for being your guiding light. He is truly a King.

By the grace of God, if I can sit back forty years from now, to review my life, I'm sure the past twenty years I've written about in this book will seem like a short chapter. It didn't seem so short while I was living it. But I know that through it all I had the choice of being the worst version of myself or the best version of myself. I am happy that I chose the best Mashonda.

I chose the best when I started to let go of all the ideas I had created along the way of how things were "supposed" to be. I pray that you will never allow heaviness to encircle your heart, that you will know the power of surrender, and that you will always embrace what the universe has in store for you. These were hard-won lessons I learned. But I was fueled by the belief that Mum, your great-grandmother, embedded in me: "Everything you will ever need is already right inside of you." This is also your truth.

Use your powers to give yourself permission to fly. Give the people you love the permission to fly. That's true love. Selfless love. Love that lives on forever.

RESOURCES

Chopra, Deepak. *The Seven Spiritual Laws of Success: A Practical Guide for the Fulfillment of Your Dreams.* San Rafael, CA: Amber-Allen, 2015.

Glass, George, with David Tabatsky. *Blending Families Successfully: Helping Parents and Kids Navigate the Challenges So That Everyone Ends up Happy.* New York: Skyhorse Publishing, 2014.

McCready, Amy. *If I Have to Tell You One More Time . . . : The Revolutionary Program That Gets Your Kids to Listen Without Nagging, Reminding, or Yelling.* New York: Jeremy P. Tarcher, 2011.

Reischer, Erica. *What Great Parents Do: 75 Simple Strategies for Raising Kids Who Thrive.* New York: TarcherPerigee, 2016.

Ricci, Isolina. *Mom's House, Dad's House: Making Two Homes for Your Child.* New York: Fireside, 1997.

Siegel, Daniel J., and Mary Hartzell. *Parenting from the Inside Out: How a Deeper Self-Understanding Can Help You Raise Children Who Thrive.* New York: Jeremy P. Tarcher, 2003.

Tsabary, Shefali. *The Conscious Parent: Transforming Ourselves, Empowering Our Children.* Vancouver, Canada: Namaste Publishing, 2010.

———. *The Awakened Family: How to Raise Empowered, Resilient, and Conscious Children.* New York: Viking, 2017.

ACKNOWLEDGMENTS

My love and thanks to Cherise Fisher, my confidant: thank you for seeing beauty in every word I wrote. And to Wendy Sherman, my warrior agent, who elegantly set me up to win.

To Sara Carder, my extraordinary publisher: thank you for believing in this project from day one. Thank you to the entire team at TarcherPerigee/Penguin Random House.

I'm grateful for the voices you hear in this book: Alicia and Kasseem "Swizz" Dean Sr. Thank you for your beautiful contributions. I'm so proud of us. To Sandra Dean, Colleen Bonnick-Lewis, Sophia Chang, Sheree Zampino Fletcher, Dr. Jeff Gardere, Adam Greitzer, Misa Hylton, Emma Johnson, Amy McCready, Taharqa Patterson, Erica Reischer, Michelle Seelinger, Dr. Shefali Tsabary, Wendy Sherman, Dan Siegel, Terrie Williams, and Malik Yoba—thank you for sharing your stories and expertise.

ACKNOWLEDGMENTS

Thank you to my energy healers—Maureen Dodd, Dr. Robert Kandarjian, and Sandra Dellcioppio—for helping me remember and enhance my power. You never doubted me. You are earth angels.

And a special thank you to my extended family, friends, and colleagues who have been an essential part of the journey: my sister and brother, Melissa Tifrere and Justin Phillips, and my parents, Heather Tifrere and Winston Tifrere; Rachel Hislop who was a part of *Blend* from the moment of conception; Aisha Mundy and Anda Torres for consistently having my back, side, and front; Pamela Newkirk, and Joan and George Hornig for being guiding lights; Cowan Whitfield for your creative eye; Mark Trophy and Matthew Middleton for handling the business and being patient with me and all my questions; my beautiful circle of sisters—Marvet Britto, Patrice Lenowitz of The Nurtured Parent, Sadaf Ahmad, Ashley Noel, Fran Taylor, Lucinda Grange, Leslie Simpson, Danielle Todd, Marvet Britto, Racquel Chevremont, Nyheike Levy, and my Avenues moms who have heard me talk about this book since Kasseem was in the first grade. I'm grateful that you are all a part of my universe.

INDEX